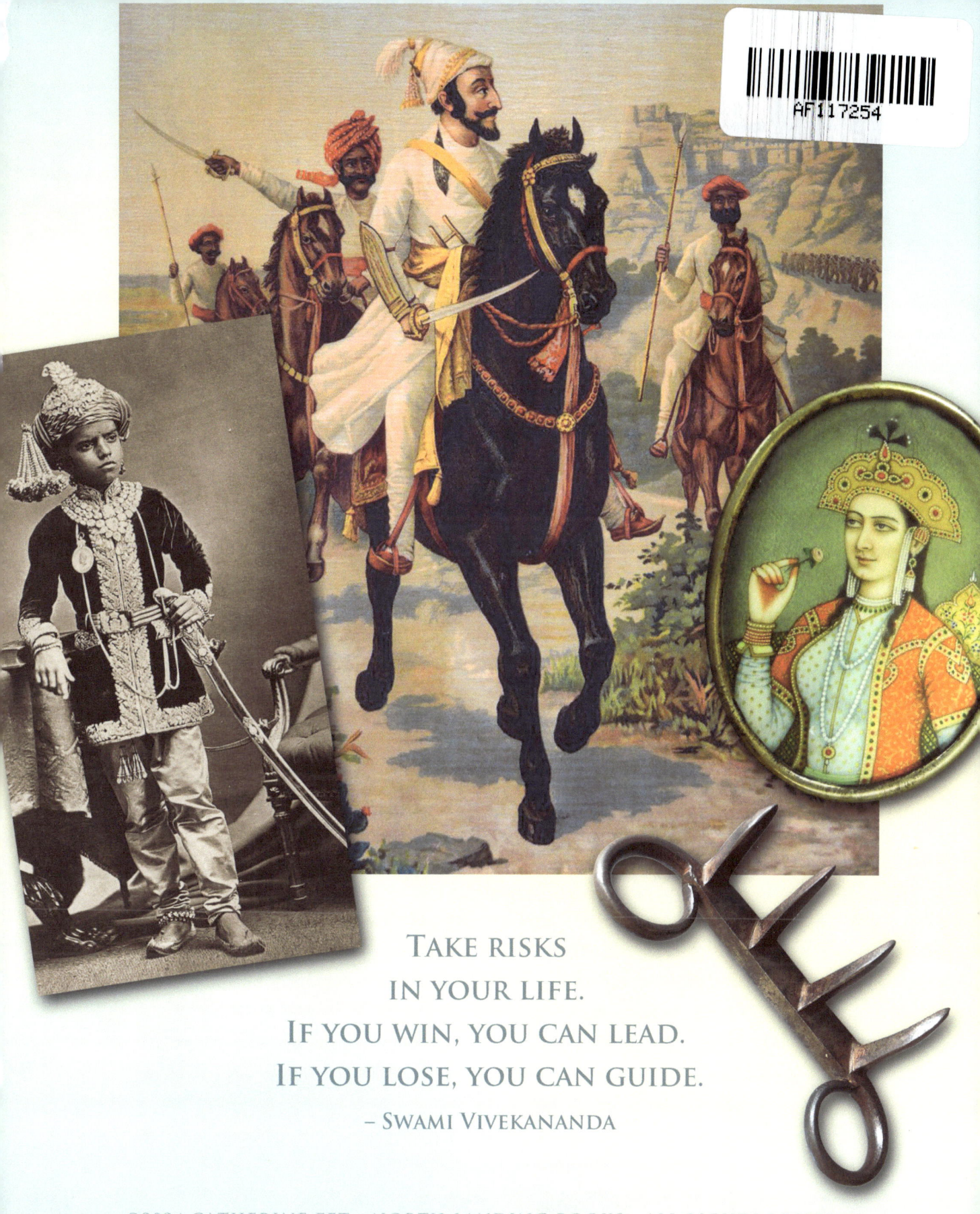

TAKE RISKS
IN YOUR LIFE.
IF YOU WIN, YOU CAN LEAD.
IF YOU LOSE, YOU CAN GUIDE.
– SWAMI VIVEKANANDA

©2024 CATHERINE FET · NORTH LANDING BOOKS · ALL RIGHTS RESERVED

Chandragupta Maurya

320 – 298 BC

Chandragupta founded the ancient Indian **Mauryan Empire** (322–185 BC) – one of the largest ever Indian kingdoms. The Mauryan Empire extended across the entire Indian subcontinent except for its southern tip. Few ancient Indian sources mention Chandragupta, but ancient Greek and Roman authors provide quite a bit of information about him, because Chandragupta's reign came soon after the Greek conqueror Alexander the Great invaded India (327 BC).

Alexander's most famous victory in India was over King Porus, whose kingdom lay in the present-day Punjab (northeast of India). The Greeks were deeply impressed with the courage and military techniques of the Indians.

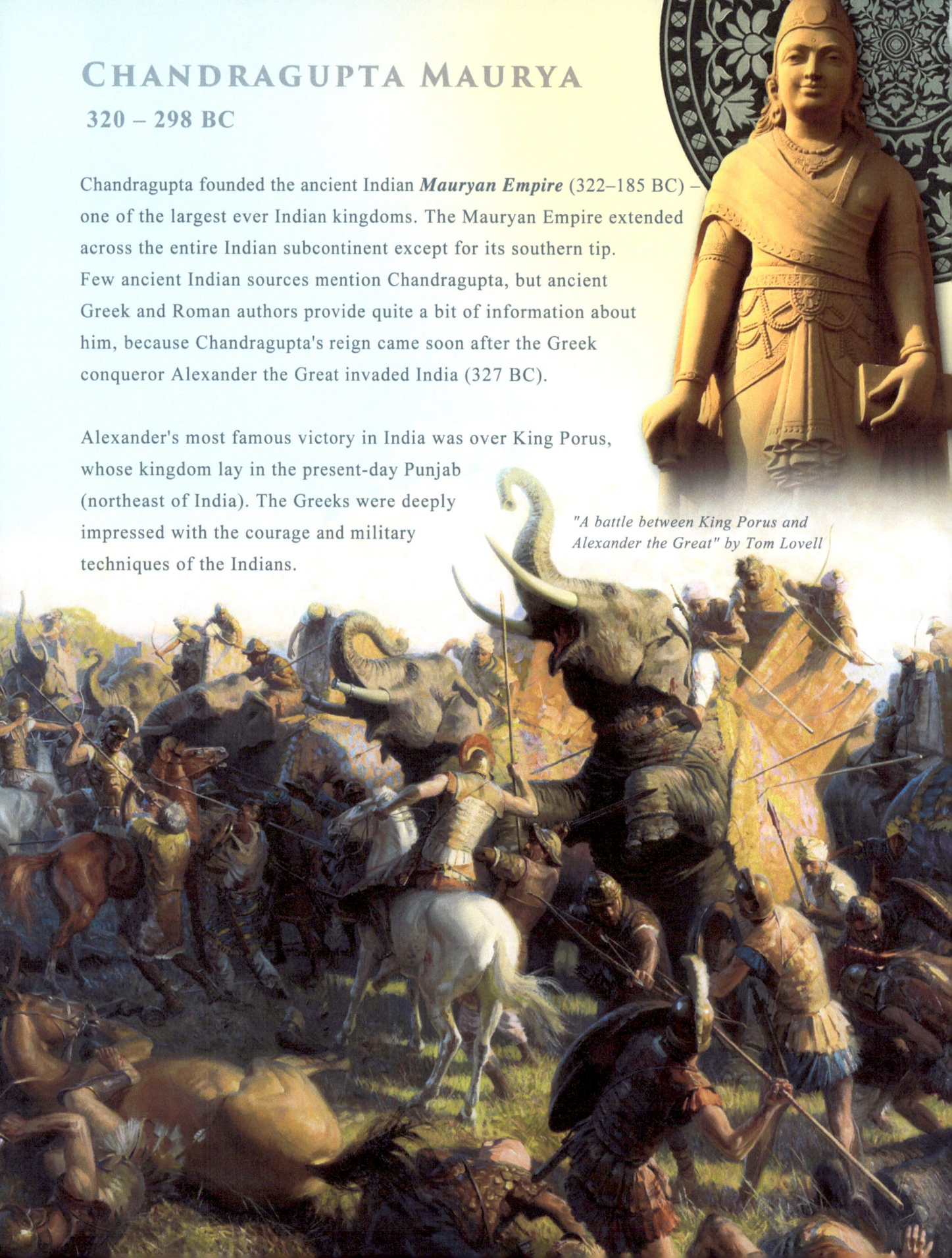

"A battle between King Porus and Alexander the Great" by Tom Lovell

Once Porus was defeated, Alexander offered to make him a *satrap* – a Persian term for a governor of a province. Alexander was also fascinated by India's battle elephants, and ordered gold rings be placed on the tusks of one particular animal that he saw display rare courage. Alexander named him Ajax in honor of one of the Greek heroes of the Trojan War from Homer's epic poem *The Iliad*. The inscription on the gold rings read, "Alexander, the son of Zeus, dedicates Ajax to Helios [the Sun god]." The victory over Porus came at great cost. Alexander's troops did not want to face another Indian army. They rebelled. So Alexander turned back toward home, leaving his satraps to govern the territories he had conquered. Four years later he died, and, as his empire fell apart, one of his generals, Seleucus Nicator ('Seleucus the Victorious') became the ruler of Alexander's Asian provinces. And that's where King Chandragupta appears in the narratives of ancient Greek historians. The source for most information about Chandragupta's reign – quoted by ancient Greek and Roman authors – was *Indica* written by Megasthenes, Seleucus' Greek ambassador to Chandragupta's court. Chandragupta came to power around 320 BC. Punjab was at the edge of his kingdom, so it was inevitable that Chandragupta's troops would one day clash with the armies of Seleucus.

How did Chandragupta become the founder of a new empire and his own Mauryan dynasty? The 12th-century Sanskrit text *The Lives of the Jain Elders* says it was Chandragupta's teacher, Chanakya, who ended up being the king-maker.

Sanskrit

Sanskrit is an ancient Indian language of the Indo-European family that was a spoken language in India in the 1st millennium BC. Eventually they stopped using it for everyday communication, and it became the language of literature, government, diplomacy, and religion. Sanskirt is viewed as the sacred language of Hinduism. It is related to such ancient Indo-European languages as Ancient Greek, Latin, and Gothic (ancient Germanic language).

Medieval **Jain** legends say that one day Chanakya helped a peacock farmer's wife who was about to give birth to a baby boy. In return he asked to be made the guardian of her son – Chandragupta. When Chandragupta grew up, Chanakya became his teacher. He admired Chandragupta's talent and courage, and, believing that he was the future emperor in the Jain monks' prophecy, advised him to take on the North Indian Nanda empire and its ruling family.

Chanakya and Chandragupta – a manuscript illustration

From Jain legends we also learn that Chanakya had a large treasure of gold. He had earned the gold practicing magic! To help Chandragupta, he used all his gold to hire soldiers for Chandragupta's army, and they marched against the Nanda capital of Pataliputra – only to be defeated. Hiding from the advancing Nanda army, one day Chanakya and Chandragupta watched a villager serve a hot dinner to her kids. One child burned his fingers, because instead of taking food from the edges of the dish where it had cooled off, he grabbed a piece from the blazing-hot middle. The villager, upset with the war ravaging her area, told her kid he was as stupid as Chanakya and Chandragupta who had attacked the Nanda capital, instead of first securing the outlying, 'cooler,' less defended regions of the empire. Wow! That villager was a real strategist! This story is a legend – likely – but *The Lives of the Jain Elders* says Chanakya and Chandragupta took this lesson to heart and started their conquest all over again – this time from the far-away, outlying areas of the Nanda kingdom. Eventually they did conquer its capital, Pataliputra.

The Vedic Period of Indian history (1500 – 500 BC)

The Vedic Period is the era of the late Bronze Age and early Iron Age in India, when the earliest Hindu sacred texts, the Vedas, were written, and the ancient form of the Hindu religion, the Vedic Hinduism, flourished.

An Ancient-Greek-style column capital (top) discsovered in the ruins of the royal palace at Pataliputra, the capital of the Mauryan Empire (3rd century BC)

Jainism

Jainism is an Indian religion that practices **asceticism** – severe self-discipline and avoidance of comfort and luxury. Jain believers also vow strict non-violence – no harm to any living beings – called **ahimsa** and follow a **lacto-vegetarian** diet (vegetables and milk products). Jains believe in reincarnation and **karma**. They say, after death a person is reborn. His behavior forms his karma – the balance of cause and effect. Depending on whether he is selfless or selfish, wise or foolish in his decisions, his life in the next incarnation may be better or worse. Jainism emerged around the 6th century BC, during the era of religious unrest, when believers who had practiced the ancient Vedic religion started looking for forms of worship that didn't require as many rituals and temple sacrifices, as these were expensive and time-consuming. Also, the warrior and merchant classes of the society felt that they were held back by the ancient **varna** or **caste** system that put **Brahmins** – the priestly class – high above everyone else. So they started supporting the new religions – **Jainism** and **Buddhism**. The most prominent teacher of Jainism in the 6th century was **Mahavira**. Both Mahavira and **Buddha** belonged to the warrior class.

A much earlier source, the *Epitome of Pompeius Trogus* written by the 2nd-century Roman author Justin, says that Chandragupta was a military commander serving 'King Nandrus' (ruler of the Nanda dynasty). According to Justin, Chandragupta didn't hesitate to criticize the king. Eventually, Nandrus took offense and sentenced him to death.

Buddhism

Buddhism emerged in India in the 6th-5th centuries BC – the same era of spiritual search and religious reform that gave rise to Jainism. The founder of Buddhism, Siddhartha Gautama, the Buddha, taught that Buddhists should seek the state of inner peace and wisdom called **nirvana** – *the 'enlightenment.' Enlightenment liberates a person from the cycle of death and rebirth. The path toward it, known as the* **Middle Way**, *is the practice of ethical behavior, meditation, and good judgement. Buddhist monks practice an ascetic life, but the rest of the Buddhist believers are told to find their own path of self-discipline.*

Chandragupta managed to escape from jail and fled into a deep forest in a remote area. One day, exhausted, he fell asleep and was awakened by a curious lion who licked his body and left without harming him. Chandragupta interpreted this event as a sign promising him the Nanda throne. Justin writes that Chandragupta "gathered a band of outlaws and incited the Indians to revolt." He also mentions that as Chandragupta was preparing for a battle against the Nanda troops, a wild elephant emerged from the jungle and kneeled in front of him, offering him a ride!

Do lions live in India?

Yes, there are lions in India! There used to be a large population of lions across the Indian subcontinent, but today only about 500-600 Asiatic lions remain. They live in the Gir National Park and Wildlife Sanctuary in Western India, their last remaining natural habitat. In the 20th century, because of hunting, the number of lions fell to less than 15. But once the Gir Forest sanctuary was established in 1965, the population of lions started growing again.

Varnas

Varnas are the original **castes** – the 4 social classes of ancient India:

Brahmins – priests, scholars, and landowners
Kshatriyas – the warrior class
Vaishyas – common people, workers, farmers
Shudras – servants

Reconstructions of Pataliputra, the capital of the Maurian Empire

Jain sources give us some details of Chandragupta's rise to the throne. One of the Nanda towns, besieged by the Mauryan troops, refused to surrender. Chanakya suspected it was guarded by a divine, supernatural force. He dressed as a beggar, sneaked into the besieged town and found out that it was protected by the seven mother goddesses of the Hindu faith whose sculptures were within the town walls. Thinking Chanakya was a traveling monk, the townspeople asked him how they could turn Chandragupta's army around and away from their town? Chanakya advised them to remove the seven goddesses from the town. They followed his advice and the town fell.

The Nanda emperor clearly lacked leadership and military talents and was disliked by his subjects. Greek and Latin authors provide us with unflattering gossip about him. Roman historian Curtius Rufus (1st century AD) wrote that the emperor's father was a barber who conspired with the Nanda queen to kill the previous Nanda king and take over the empire. "Then, under the pretense of acting as guardian to the royal children, he seized the supreme authority, put the young princes to death, and then had a child with the queen. That child became the present king who is despised by his subjects." Another Roman historian, Diodorus, describes the Nanda king as "a man of worthless character held in no respect, because he was thought to be the son of a barber." When Chandragupta captured the Nanda capital Pataliputra, he showed mercy to the defeated Nanda emperor and let him leave the city in a chariot loaded with his family's treasures. The emperor's daughter, impressed with Chandragupta's generosity, fell in love with him, and Chandragupta married her.

Having won the Nanda throne, Chandragupta "was preparing for war against Alexander's governors" in Punjab, writes Justin. Seleucus Nicator, who had taken over Alexander's Asian provinces, learned about this and rushed to India, but it was already too late. "Seleucus crossed into India," continues Justin, "which, following Alexander's death, had shaken from its shoulders the yoke of servitude [= slavery] and put to death his governors. The man responsible for this liberation was Sandrocottus [the Greek name for Chandragupta]. However, after his victory he had turned the liberty they had gained back into servitude, because, having seized power, he (Chandragupta) himself, began to enslave the people whom he had saved from foreign domination." Justin refers to Chandragupta's push to expand his new empire across North India – from Bengal to Afghanistan – and also deep toward the south of the Indian subcontinent.

Seleucus was not about to abandon Alexander's Indian provinces without a battle. He marched east. On the banks of the Indus River Chandragupta's army of 600,000 men stood waiting for him. Greek historian Appian (2nd century AD) writes in his *Roman History* that Seleucus "crossed the Indus and waged war on Sandrocottus, king of the Indians, who lived on the banks of that river, until they came to an agreement with each other and sealed it with a marriage" between their family members. Roman historian Strabo (62 BC – AD 24) says that Seleucus Nicator gave to Chandragupta all the territories conquered by Alexander, and received in exchange 500 war elephants! It was the deal of the century, because these elephants won for Seleucus the Battle of Ipsus he later fought against his rivals among Alexander the Great's generals.

Arthashastra ("Economics"), the ancient Indian book on economics and political science, supposedly written by Chanakya himself, says that Chandragupta's reign was prosperous and tolerant. While practicing Vedic Hinduism himself, Chandragupta welcomed other faiths, such as Buddhism and Jainism, and held lavish festivals on religious holidays. The Jain legends suggest that at some point Chandragupta converted to Jainism and left his throne to his son. Many historians, however, believe it to be unlikely, because Jain legends all date to a much later era. In contrast, the ancient Greek and Roman sources describe Chandragupta hunting and participating in rituals that included animal sacrifices – incompatible with the principle of *ahimsa* – nonviolence towards living beings – strictly observed by the Jain believers.

Seleucus Nicator on one of his coins;
War elephants in the Battle of the Hydaspes
(Alexander the Great vs King Porus)
by Nicolaes Pietersz Berchem

The Mauryan capital Pataliputra was destroyed by invasions – possibly in the 6th century – and disappeared. It had stood at the confluence (merging) of the Ganges and the Son rivers, but over the centuries these rivers changed their course, and the location of Pataliputra was forgotten. It was rediscovered by archaeologists in the late 19th century.

In *The Early History of India* (1908) English historian Vincent A. Smith, describes the royal court in Pataliputra (based on archaeological discoveries and books by Indian, Roman, and Greek authors): "Here the imperial court was maintained with barbaric and luxurious ostentation. Basins and goblets of gold, some measuring six feet in width, richly carved tables and chairs, vessels of Indian copper set with precious stones, and gorgeous embroidered robes were to be seen in abundance, and contributed to the brilliance of the public ceremonies. When the king showed himself in public on state occasions he was carried in a golden *palanquin*, adorned with tassels of pearls, and was clothed in fine muslin embroidered with purple and gold. When making short journeys he rode on horseback, but when traveling longer distances he rode on an elephant with a golden harness. Combats of animals were a favorite entertainment, as they still are at the courts of native princes, and the king took delight in witnessing the fights of bulls, rams, elephants, rhinoceroses, and other animals. Gladiatorial contests between men were also exhibited."

*A **palanquin** - a seat carried on two horizontal poles by four or six bearers*

And here is how Greek geographer Strabo described the Mauryan capital and the local customs in his book *Geography* (Book XV, sections 36-55): "At the confluence of the Ganges and of another river is situated Pataliputra... It is in the shape of a parallelogram, surrounded by a wooden wall pierced with openings through which arrows may be shot. In front is a ditch, which serves the purpose of defense and of a sewer for the city. The people in whose country the city is situated are the most distinguished of all the tribes... All the Indians are frugal in their mode of life, especially at a military camp. Theft is very rare among them... Megasthenes says that none of the Indians employ slaves... In contrast to their frugality in other things, they indulge in ornament. They wear dresses decorated with gold and precious stones, and multi-colored robes, and are attended by persons following them with umbrellas. Since they value beauty so highly, they take care of every detail that enhances their looks. They respect alike truth and virtue, and do not give any special privilege to the old, unless they possess superior wisdom... The king does not sleep during the day-time, and at night he is obliged from time to time to change his bed, for fear of being killed."

Ashoka the Great
304 – 232 BC

Ashoka the Great was a grandson of Chandragupta. His empire covered most of the Indian subcontinent from present-day Bangladesh to Kabul and Kandahar in present-day Afghanistan. Most of what we know about Ashoka comes from inscriptions engraved on stone – on pillars, rocks, and cave walls – during his reign, and from the much later Buddhist sources that collected legends about his life. The Buddhist sources are generally believed to be somewhat unreliable. At some point during his reign Ashoka converted to Buddhism, so the Buddhist legends all focus on the contrast between how evil and violent Ashoka was before his conversion and how wise and charitable he became after the conversion. As a result, they clearly exaggerate both his crimes and his achievements.

Ashoka's "lion" pillars

Let us first take a look at Ashoka's own reports about his life engraved in stone – his *edicts* (edict = an official announcement or order). From Ashoka's edicts we learn that he had a few brothers and sisters, at least two wives (because the inscriptions mention his "Second Queen"), and four sons whom he appointed governors of his empire's provinces. Every year Ashoka celebrated the anniversary of his coronation by releasing prisoners from jails. One of his Pillar Edicts reads, "During the period that has elapsed since I was anointed king – twenty-six years – prisoners were released from jails twenty-five times." The king organized festivals for the residents of his capital. At these events townspeople were served meat dishes and watched music, dance, and wrestling shows.

We know what dishes Ashoka liked most – venison (deer meat) and peacocks! In his Rock Edict I, engraved after Ashoka had converted to Buddhism, he mentions animals killed for his dinners and promises to become a vegetarian: "When this document of *Dharma* (Buddhist teaching) was written, only three animals were killed for curry, namely, two peacocks and only one deer, but even that deer – not regularly. These three animals will not from now on be killed." What did the great emperor do for fun? "While previous kings went hunting for pleasure, or enjoyed music, feasts, and magic shows," says one of the inscriptions, "I have replaced all that with pilgrimages to the holy Buddhist sites." For example, Ashoka visited the place where Buddha achieved enlightenment, the *Bodhi Tree*. This occurred in the 8th year of Ashoka's reign – that's when he converted to Buddhism.

A "rock edict" by Emperor Ashoka

What prompted Ashoka's conversion? This happened after he conquered Kalinga, a princedom on the Bay of Bengal. So many people perished during this invasion, the tragedy was so massive, that Ashoka was struck with a sense of grief and remorse, and felt that his whole life was on the wrong track. In one of his post-conquest edicts, Ashoka mentions the enemy casualties: "150,000 were carried away as captives, 100,000 were killed in battle, and many times more died [of starvation]."

Of course, on top of that there were thousands of Ashoka's own troops who perished in that war. "His Majesty feels remorse on account of the conquest of the Kalinga," continues Ashoka in his edict, "because during the subjugation of a previously unconquered country, slaughter, death, and captivity occur. His Majesty feels profound sorrow and regret about this..." Ashoka sought spiritual guidance that promoted non-violence. He joined the Buddhist community, and 2 years later took the vows of a Buddhist monk. Chinese traveler Yijing, who visited India in the 7th century, wrote that he had seen the statues of Ashoka representing him as wearing a monk's robe.

In his edicts Ashoka lays down his philosophy as a ruler: "All men are my children, and, just as I desire for my children that they may obtain every kind of welfare and happiness both in this and the next world, so do I desire this for all men... There is no higher work than the welfare of the whole world. And that's why whatever effort I make is to be free from debt to the living creatures and to bring them happiness here and to help them gain heaven in the next world. For this purpose have I caused this document of Dharma to be engraved, in order that it may endure for a long time and that my sons and grandsons may similarly work tirelessly for the welfare of the whole world. This, however, is difficult to carry out without the utmost effort."

His inscriptions detail various projects Ashoka undertook to improve the life of his subjects. He instructed his government to plant thousands of "shade-giving and fruit-bearing trees," to dig wells, to build "rest houses" along the roads, and to cultivate medicinal herbs and roots. Ashoka also believed in protecting the sanctity of animal life. He banned killing any animals not raised for food. Hunting tigers became illegal in his kingdom.

And now let's explore the legends about Ashoka the Great. The legends tell us that, growing up, Ashoka wasn't a good-looking kid. His dad, the Mauryan emperor, thought he was ugly because his skin was rough and scarred. Everybody at the court thought that Ashoka's brother, Vitashoka, would be appointed the heir to the throne, but when the boys' mother, the queen, asked a famous Buddhist monk about the destiny of her two sons, the monk said the throne would belong to Ashoka, and immediately left the Mauryan lands to avoid punishment for his prophecy.

At some point the town of Taxila rebelled against the Mauryan emperor. Ashoka's dad sent Ashoka to suppress the rebellion, but didn't give him enough weapons to succeed. Ashoka didn't hold this against his father, and declared that the gods would provide him with weapons. Indeed, just as Ashoka approached Taxila, the earth opened, and divine beings emerged from its depth carrying all the weapons and supplies he needed.

The Taxila townspeople saw Ashoka approach and walked out to meet him. They explained that they had rebelled against the emperor's corrupt governor, not against the emperor himself. Ashoka made peace with them and returned home to the Mauryan capital Pataliputra. When Ashoka's dad grew old, he offered the throne to Vitashoka, but Ashoka conspired with the royal ministers and counselors that they should persuade the king to pass the crown to Ashoka. The king refused. In response Ashoka said that he would be crowned anyway – not by the old emperor, but by the gods themselves. Indeed, gods appeared and crowned him, and as the crown touched his head, his father died. Appalled by this, Vitashoka raised an army and besieged Pataliputra, but Ashoka found some giants and had them guard the gates! Eventually Vitashoka perished and Ashoka became king. As a ruler, he was a real tyrant. One day 500 of his ministers and counselors dared to criticize his orders. Enraged, Ashoka drew his sword and chopped off the heads of those rebels – all 500 of them... Hey, it's a legend! Next, Ashoka learned that the women in his palace – his wives and court ladies – were laughing at him because he was ugly. To express their scorn for him, they cut all the flowers and leaves off of an *ashoka tree* (a tropical tree with bright red flowers) in the palace garden. Ashoka had all these women burned alive... coincidentally, there were also 500 of them!

Where history stops, legend takes over!

Stupa

In Buddhism, a stupa is a structure that contains relics (the remains) of Buddhist monks or nuns and is used as a place of meditation.

Below: The Great Stupa in the village of Sanchi, the birthplace of Ashoka's wife; Flowers of ashoka tree
Right: Lion Capital (top) of one of Ashoka's pillars

Ashoka also built a huge prison which he called "Hell" and hired a nasty criminal as an executioner. He swore that not a single man who ever enters that prison should leave it alive. From the outside, however, the prison looked like a palace. Occasionally townspeople wandered into its gates drawn by curiosity – only to be tortured and killed. One day, a holy man, the Buddhist monk Samudra, walked through the gates of the prison. The executioner grabbed him and threw him into a cauldron of boiling oil and filth. But the holy man didn't perish! The burning liquid and the fire could not harm him. The executioner called Ashoka, and seeing this miracle, Ashoka converted to Buddhism, demolished the prison, and executed the executioner.

The state emblem and the flag of the Republic of India

The state emblem of India is the famous Lion Capital of Ashoka – the head of a column erected by Ashoka in Sarnath, India, in 250 BC and excavated in 1905. The lions on the column represented power, courage, pride, and confidence. They sit on a cylindrical base with the relief images of a horse, a bull, a lion, and an elephant. It's likely that these animals symbolized the reign of Ashoka in the "four quarters of the world." Another image on the base of the Lion Capital is the so-called "Ashoka Chakra" – a wheel symbol that now appears in the center of the national flag of India. This wheel is a sacred Buddhist symbol representing the "wheel of time." Its 24 spokes stand for the 24 qualities of human character Buddha's followers should seek to develop:
Love, Courage, Patience, Charity, Magnanimity (generosity), Goodness, Faith, Gentleness, Selflessness, Self-Control, Self-Sacrifice, Truthfulness, Righteousness, Justice, Mercy, Graciousness, Humility, Loyalty, Sympathy, Spiritual Knowledge, Forgiveness, Honesty, Eternity, Hope.

These symbols of the Mauryan Empire era were adopted by India in 1950 as emblems of its national identity to affirm the principles of peace and tolerance – the lessons of Ashoka's reign.

सत्यमेव जयते

The state motto of India

"Truth Alone Triumphs" – in Sanskrit. These words come from **Upanishads** (part of the Vedas, the holy books of Hinduism).

The state flower of India

The state flower of India is the lotus – 'padma,' or 'kamala' in Sanskrit

HARSHA
590 – 647

Harshavardhana, or Harsha, was the ruler of the Kingdom of Kannauj in North India. Most of what we know about Harsha's life comes from one of two sources: the *Harshacharita* ("The Life of Harsha") by Harsha's court poet Banabhatta, and *Records of the Western Regions* by the Chinese traveler Xuanzang, a Buddhist monk who visited Harsha's court.

By the 6th century, the great Indian Gupta Empire founded by Chandragupta Maurya collapsed and fell apart because of infighting between regional rulers and attacks by the Huns, nomadic tribes from

"Harsha saves his sister" from the cover of "Harsha" by the famous Indian comic book pubisher Amar Chitra Katha

the Eurasian **steppes** (= grasslands). India split again into numerous kingdoms and princedoms. Harsha was the second son of the king of Thanesar in North India. He had a brother, Rajyavardhana, and a sister, Rajyashri, who was married to the king of Maukhari, another North Indian kingdom. When Harsha was 15, the Huns invaded his region. The King of Thanesar raised an army to defend his land. Harsha's elder brother Rajyavardhana commanded the assault troops that went ahead of the Thanesar army, while Harsha – at 15! – commanded units protecting the flanks and the rear of the army. The Huns were crushed, but Harsha's dad became ill during this campaign and died.

Rajyavardhana was crowned king of Thanesar. All went well until the Kingdom of Maukhari, where Harsha's sister Rajyashri was queen, suffered an attack by its neighbor, King Devagupta of Malwa. Rajyashri's husband, the king, was killed in battle, and Rajyashri was captured and locked up in jail in Malwa. Harsha's brother Rajyavardhana declared war on Devagupta, and invaded his kingdom with a force of 10,000 cavalry fighters. Devagupta was defeated and killed, but Rajyavardhana failed to rescue his sister, and was soon betrayed and killed. His ally, the King of Gauda from

Eastern Bengal, had been bribed by the Malwa ruling family. He invited Rajyavardhana to a meeting and murdered him there. When the royal advisors and ministers came to Harsha with the news that he was to be crowned king, Harsha refused to take the throne. He was only 16, and absolutely not interested in ruling a kingdom. But then he realized that if he didn't lead an army to save his sister, nobody would. So he agreed to become king. As Harsha's troops marched toward Gauda, the news came that the King of Gauda, dreading Harsha's revenge, released Rajyashri from a jail in Malwa. Word was, she was hiding in the woods with a few court ladies. Harsha rushed to look for her. Meanwhile, Rajyashri who had lost her husband, and had only then learned about the death of her elder brother, was deeply depressed and decided to end her life. She ordered her servants to light a huge bonfire, planning to throw herself into the flames. Fortunately, at the very last moment, Harsha found her camp and prevented the tragedy.

Once the rescue of his sister was accomplished, Harsha sought to avenge the death of his brother. He turned the Thanesar army against Gauda and was victorious. But Harsha's conquest didn't stop there.

From "Harsha" – a comic book by Amar Chitra Katha

Harsha's silver coin

He kept capturing princedoms of Northern India until his kingdom grew into a vast and powerful empire. Chinese traveler Xuanzang wrote that "he waged incessant warfare, until, in six years, he had conquered the five Indias [kingdoms/regions]. Then, having enlarged his territory, he increased his army, bringing the number of war elephants up to 60,000, and the cavalry to 100,000, and reigned in peace for thirty years without raising a weapon."

As a ruler and administrator of his empire, Harsha was respected and much praised. Like Ashoka, he built hospitals and rest houses on the roads, and traveled to even the most remote corners of his kingdom just to see the beauty and the vastness of India with his own eyes. The only persistent problem during his reign were highway robberies. Xuanzang traveled around India for 14 years and was robbed a number of times, even though the laws of Harsha's empire prescribed severe punishments for this type of crime, such as chopping off criminals' noses, hands, and feet.

Harsha surrounded himself with poets and writers, and is credited for having written three famous plays in Sanskrit – *Ratnavali, Nagananda,* and *Priyadarsika*. One day Harsha called on the poets of his kingdom, asking them to contribute their works to a collection that would demonstrate "the best poetry ever written." Out of all the poems submitted for this project, 500 were selected as the best and performed in public. Harsha also helped grow schools, including the Buddhist Nalanda University in Bihar, believed to be the first residential university in the world. It had an observatory and a spectacular library. The money to support the university came from 200 villages gifted to it by various rulers, so the instruction, boarding and lodging (food and a place to sleep) were free. At Nalanda University around 3000 students studied religious subjects, logic, grammar, astronomy, medicine, and art. The classes were taught in Sanskrit. To be admitted, you had to take an entrance exam that was famous for being extremely hard. Scholars from all over India and other countries came to Nalanda to exchange knowledge.

Ruins of the Nalanda University library. It was said to have hundreds of thousands of books in its collection. It was burned around 1200 during the conquest of Bihar by Afghan Islamic rulers.

Harsha's dad had worshiped the Sun, following the ancient Hindu beliefs of his ancestors. Harsha kept his family's faith, but also respected other religions. Later in life he became interested in Buddhism, prohibited the slaughter of animals, and built many Buddhist stupas and monasteries along the Ganges River. When Chinese pilgrim Xuanzang reached Harsha's royal court, Harsha was impressed with the way he discussed and interpreted the principles of Buddhism, and became Xuanzang's friend and protector. To honor Xuanzang, Harsha called an assembly of princes, nobles, and the scholars of his empire. Twenty kings, 4000 Buddhist monks, and 3000 Jain and Hindu scholars arrived on the banks of the Ganges where Emperor Harsha built a palace for himself and guest houses for visitors. Harsha also built a tower 100 ft. (30 meters) high. Every morning a procession of guests and Harsha's courtiers carried a gold statue of Buddha under a richly-decorated canopy from the royal palace to the tower. Harsha himself put on a costume of Sakra, a heavenly ruler of the Buddhist legends, and went ahead of the procession throwing pearls, gold and silver coins, and flowers on the way. The royal guests rode elephants. 100 elephants carried musicians and drummers, and 500 battle elephants followed the procession along with Harsha's guards. After this ceremony, Harsha had hundreds of silk robes decorated with precious gems laid in front of the golden Buddha as a gift. Next, he invited everyone to be present at a discussion of Buddhist doctrine held by scholars and monks.

This routine was repeated every day for a month, until it was disrupted by a fire that suddenly blazed in a Buddhist monastery on the river bank. As royal guards and some of the guests rushed to the monastery to put out the fire, Harsha went up a stupa next to the monastery building to see what was going on. There he was ambushed by an assassin who tried to stab him with a knife. Harsha escaped, and his guards quickly tracked down and captured the assassin. The criminal confessed that he had been hired by some Brahminist priests upset at the king for promoting Buddhism. He had set the monastery on fire to cause panic and confusion that would enable him to get close to the emperor.

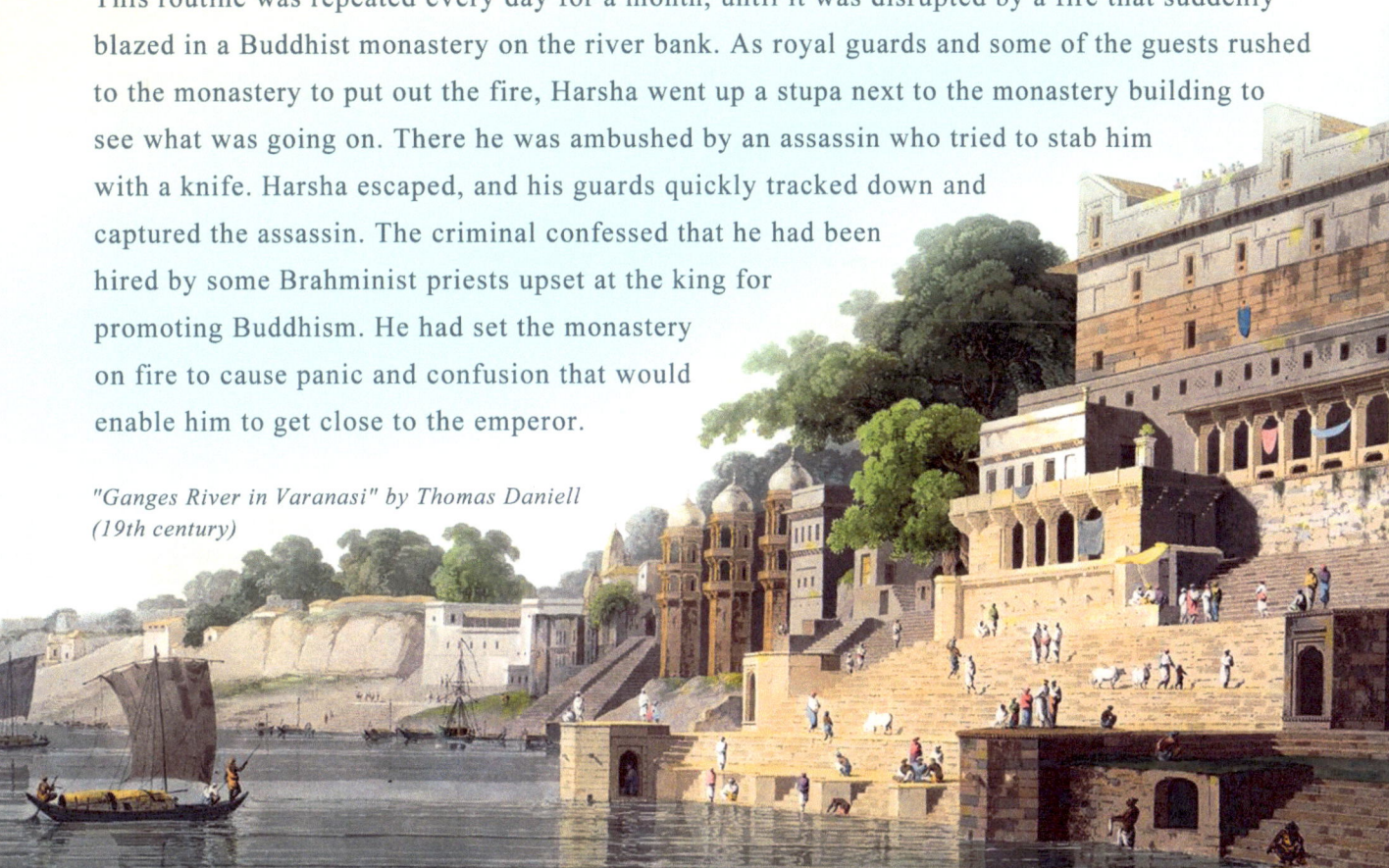

"Ganges River in Varanasi" by Thomas Daniell (19th century)

The Ganges River

The River Ganges flows from the Himalayan Mountains across Northern India and empties out into Bay of Bengal. Many capitals of ancient Indian empires, such as Pataliputra, Kannauj, and Delhi, stood on its banks. In Hinduism the Ganges is viewed as a sacred river, so its water is used in many rituals. Pilgrims who come to the Ganges River scoop water in their cupped hands or in a bowl and pour it back out into the river saying a prayer. The Ganges water is sprinkled on clothes and food, and is given to the sick. Pilgrims who come to bathe in the Ganges River float offerings of flowers, fruit, and oil lamps on its waters, and take the sealed bottles of the Ganges water to keep at home for good luck and healing.

Xuanzang also described a festival of charity Emperor Harsha held in Prayagraj, Northern India, every 5 years. There was a place in Prayagraj called "the arena of charitable offerings," wrote Xuanzang. In ancient days kings from across India came there to share their wealth with the poor. Emperor Harsha came to Prayagraj bringing loads of treasures and held a ceremony that lasted for 3 months. People of all faiths were invited.

"On the first day they installed the image of Buddha there," reported Xuanzang, "and gave away precious items and clothing of the first quality. The second day they installed the image of Aditya [the Sun god in ancient Hinduism] and gave away things and clothing that cost half the amount of the donations given away the previous day. On the third day they installed the image of Ishvara [Hindu deity] and distributed gifts as on the second day. On the fourth day they gave gifts to 10,000 Buddhist monks, each receiving 100 pieces of gold, one pearl, one cotton garment, various drinks and meats, flowers and perfumes. For the next twenty days gifts were given to the Brahminist pilgrims. For the month that followed gifts were made to the poor, the orphans, and the destitute. By this time the king ran out of the gold and goods saved for charity over five years. He didn't give away the horses, elephants, and military equipment necessary for maintaining order and protecting the kingdom. But of other treasures, nothing remained. The king even gave away his own gems and goods, his clothing, necklaces, earrings, and bracelets... All being given away, he asked his sister to get him some ordinary second-hand clothes, and having put them on, he worshiped the Buddha images, and was filled with joy, holding his hands in a prayerful gesture... Once the ceremony was over, the kings [from the provinces of Harsha's empire] bought back from the people royal [Harsha's] necklaces, jewels, and court clothes he had given away, and brought them back to the emperor. But only a few days later these same things were given away in charity again!" And that was the end of the charity festival. Harsha told Xuanzang that he had already held 5 such celebrations.

The event described by Xuanzang was the last for Harsha. He died in 647, leaving no heir to his throne. One of the governors of imperial provinces, Arunasva, seized the throne, but his rule didn't last. His troops attacked the Chinese embassy, killed some of the Chinese staff and plundered their property. The king of Tibet who was married to a Chinese princess sent an army to rescue the Chinese diplomats. A Chinese invasion followed, and Harsha's empire fell apart.

Triveni Sangam

The Indian city of Prayagraj is the site of the confluence of the Ganges and the Yamuna rivers. Ancient legends said that there had once been a third river that joined the Ganges and Yamuna at Prayagraj – the Sarasvati River. So the Hindu believers call the place where these rivers met Triveni Sangam – "the confluence of three rivers" and consider it sacred. Many believe that bathing in Triveni Sangam can wash away a person's sins and stop the cycle of rebirth, opening the way to heaven.

"Pilgrims in Prayagraj" by Achille Beltrame (early 20th century)

RAZIA SULTAN
1205 – 1240

Razia Sultan was the Queen, or "Sultana," of the Muslim Sultanate of Delhi for 4 years (1236 – 1240). The Delhi Sultanate was established around 1206 and lasted for about 300 years. At its height it stretched across most of the Indian subcontinent. The ruling class of the sultanate consisted of the descendants of Afghans, Arabs, Persians, and Turks. Persian was the preferred language at the royal court in Delhi. Indian converts to Islam sought to adopt Arab and Persian customs to rise in the civil or military ranks of the empire.

Indian movie star Hema Malini playing Razia Sultan in the 1983 film "Razia Sultan"

The Islamic conquest of India begins

Soon after the death of prophet Muhammad, the founder of Islam, the Arab kingdoms that adopted Islam started a series of conquests to spread their faith to new regions. Egypt and Syria were conquered first. Then the Islamic world spread to North Africa, Spain, and Persia, and reached the Kabul River in present-day Afghanistan. The conquest of North-Western India started in the early 8th century, as the Umayyad **Caliphate** (caliphate = muslim kingdom) attacked the Hindu kingdom of Sindh (in present-day Pakistan) ruled by King Dahir of Aror.

Dahir repelled the first wave of the invasion, but his allies, the Buddhist rulers of neighboring towns, chose to surrender to the Umayyads rather than fight. Next, Dahir was cornered in his capital city of Aror. According to the 13th-century Persian text describing the fall of Sindh, Dahir made his last stand in front of the gates of Aror. The first attack was fought off, but then Dahir's elephant was wounded and rushed off the battlefield carrying the king with him. Thinking that Dahir had perished, the defenders of Aror retreated in panic and shut the gates of the city. Dahir fell on the battlefield, fighting with desperate courage. His son took the decision to abandon the city and fled, but his wife, the Queen of Aror and the remains of the Sindh army defended the city until they ran out of arrows – and eventually ran out of food.

Facing the prospect of humiliation, torture, and execution by the caliphate, the queen and the citizens of Aror decided to die free. They lit a fire on the fortress square, burned all their treasures, and then the women, including the queen, put on their best clothes and threw themselves into the flames. All the men of Aror, armed with their remaining weapons, stones, and torches, flung wide the fortress gates, marched out and perished under the onslaught of the enemy.

Hema Malini as Razia Sultan

Razia's dad, Iltutmish, was one of the **Mamluk** kings. Mamluks were slave soldiers – mostly from Turkey and the Caucasus mountains – who fought for Islamic caliphates during the era of the Muslim conquests. Captured and sold into slavery as a kid, Iltutmish was a talented military commander. He was freed from slavery and eventually raised to the position of a provincial governor and royal advisor by a Muslim sultan of the Ghor region in present-day Afghanistan. When the sultan died, Iltutmish conspired with **Turkic** nobles at the court and seized the throne. He was the first sultan to set up his capital in Delhi, so he is considered to be the founder of the Delhi Sultanate. Iltutmish also became the first Muslim ruler to choose a woman as his heir. He had a few sons, but in his opinion none of them qualified to wear a crown. So when he left his capital on military campaigns, he put his daughter Razia in charge of his government. Historical accounts of his reign quote him saying, "My sons are incapable of leading, and for that reason I have decided that it is my daughter who should reign after me."

Turkic Peoples

Turkic Peoples are inhabitants of Eurasia who speak Turkic languages. Among them are such ethnic groups as Turks, Uzbeks, Azeris (from Azerbaijan), Kazakhs, Turkmens, Tatars, Uyghurs, and many others.

This choice seemed so unacceptable to most of Iltutmish's advisors and ministers, that when the king died, they ignored his will and crowned his eldest son, Ruknuddin. But Ruknuddin had no interest in ruling his kingdom. He spent all day watching dance shows and magicians, and wasted enormous amounts of gold giving gifts to his favorite dancers and clowns. Meanwhile the kingdom was actually being run by his mom, Shah Turkan,

"Sultana Razia" – a comic book by Amar Chitra Katha

who had started as a Turkic slave brought to the sultan's palace to cook and clean, and ended up one of Iltutmish's wives and the manager of his **harem** (the women's part of the palace). Shah Turkan was a ruthless and cruel woman, focused entirely on revenge – jailing and executing anyone who had ever mistreated her in her slave days. She also started eliminating her son's rivals – her husband's kids by other wives. When she threw one of Ruknuddin's half-brothers into jail, and then had him blinded, and then had him executed, the other brothers started an uprising. To fight with his rebellious siblings, Ruknuddin left Delhi. Meanwhile his mom, Shah Turkan, sent her guards to capture and kill Razia. It was Friday, and all the capital's nobles and hundreds of common folk assembled at the city's main mosque for the Friday night prayer. Realizing that she was being hunted by Shah Turkan's men, Razia rushed to the mosque and addressed the people present there, calling on them to overthrow Ruknuddin. This time around, the court nobles and ministers, and even the **wazir** (prime minister) had wisened up and supported Razia. An angry crowd gathered by the royal palace, stormed it, and seized Shah Turkan. As a result, after a mere 7 months in power, Ruknuddin was overthrown – and executed. A few months later his mother Shah Turkan was also put to death.

Many of the families who supported Razia were the same Turkic nobles who had once supported her dad. They expected her to sit on the throne and leave all the decisions to them. But they were in for a surprise. Razia took charge. She commanded her realm with an iron grip and got into every detail of her government's work. At her palace, Razia appeared daily on her throne listening to her ministers' reports, receiving ambassadors, and revising the laws. At first Razia kept issuing coins with her father's name, but soon Iltutmish's name on the coins was replaced with an inscription: "Pillar of Women, Queen forever, Sultana Razia daughter of Shams ud-Din Iltutmish." At the beginning of her reign Razia observed the rules of modesty prescribed for Muslim women of that era. She wore a veil, all her guards were female, and when she sat on her throne, there was a screen that separated her from the men of the court and the visitors. But after a few months on the throne Razia discarded the veil and the screen, replaced her female guards with men, started wearing mens' clothes, and even showed up in public in battle armor riding an elephant! Still, for now, Razia's advisors praised her judgment, and on the streets of Delhi crowds cheered when she rode by.

There was, however, one thing the Delhi court held against Razia. She seemed to be paying too much attention to her Master of the Horse, Jamal ud-Din Yaqut, who oversaw the royal stables. She kept showering him with gifts and allowed him to lift her onto her horse. Burning with jealousy, Razia's courtiers whispered behind her back that it was a violation of the rules of modesty. Some went so far as to suggest he was Razia's boyfriend. They also couldn't get over the fact that Yaqut was a slave from Abyssinia (Ethiopia)! And it wasn't the first time Razia gave high court positions to 'foreigners.' Most government officials in the sultanate were of Turkic or Persian origin, but Razia didn't trust them and started to rely more and more on 'foreigners' and local Indians. Razia knew that the men competing for her attention at the court were enraged by the favor she showed to her Master of the Horse, but she didn't realize that her enemies were using gossip about her and Yaqut to provoke a rebellion. One day Razia announced that Yaqut would be raised to the rank of Amir al-Umara (Emir of the Emirs = Prince of the Princes), the top military commander in the sultanate, elevating him over all other officials in the kingdom. That was a blow the Delhi nobles couldn't bear. It was a major insult, especially given the fact that a few military campaigns waged by Razia against rebels in her sultanate's provinces had all failed, and now she was about to appoint "an African slave" to teach her commanders how to win battles!

One of the first to openly rebel was Malik Altunia, the governor of Bhatinda province of the sultanate, located in present-day Punjab. Altunia started his career as a slave of Razia's dad who purchased him when Altunia was a kid. According to rumors that circulated at the court,

Razia and Jamal ud-Din Yaqut from the cover of a vinyl record with the music featured in the 1983 Indian movie "Razia Sultan"

he and Razia had grown up together and he had always been in love with her. Gossipers believed he had even hoped to marry her. For 4 years of Razia's reign Altunia had been one of her most loyal supporters. When he was at the court in Delhi, Razia's enemies didn't dare to attack her. Only when he had left to become the governor of Bhatinda, did conspirators start preparing to overthrow Razia. The fact that Altunia had given up on her and rebelled was especially bad news.

When the rebellion broke out, fearing Delhi would be besieged, Razia and Yaqut left the city to meet Altunia's troops in an open field. But Razia's soldiers sympathized with Altunia who had risen from a slave to a successful military commander. They didn't want to go into battle led by a woman and her "foreigner boyfriend." So most of them defected (switched sides) to Altunia. The remnants of Razia's army were defeated, Yaqut was killed, and Razia was taken prisoner. In Delhi, Razia's half brother, Muiz ud-Din Bahram, declared himself the sultan and awarded all the new government positions to his friends. Malik Altunia reached out to him asking to be included in the government since he was the one who had put Razia on her knees, but Bahram ignored him. Altunia realized that his rebellion had gained nothing but disaster both for him and Razia, and decided to see Razia and apologize.

African slaves in India

Slave trade between Africa and India was run by Arab slave traders who purchased prisoners of war from East African tribes and exchanged them for luxurious cloth, spices, ivory, gems, and other valuable goods from India. Indian rulers were eager to buy Africans, because they were considered to be excellent warriors.

In captivity Razia lived in a luxurious apartment, was allowed to go to the mosque on Friday nights, and was treated like royalty. So when Altunia showed up to talk to her, she quickly forgave him, and in no time they agreed to become allies and seek to return the sultan's throne to Razia. More than that, a few weeks later they got married! But Razia was not destined to return to Delhi.

AND AT BHATINDA, AS THE WEEKS PASSED, ALTUNIA UNDERSTOOD.
I WAS A JEALOUS FOOL TO HAVE DOUBTED YOUR LOVE! FORGIVE ME, RAZIA.

Altunia's army was defeated in a battle against Razia's brother. Razia and Malik Altunia fled toward the North West of India. Over there, they were robbed and killed by local tribes people who had no idea who they were. Razia Sultan's life story – daring, tragic, and romantic – became the plot of movies, novels, and comic books. She remains one of the historical figures of India most widely celebrated in modern pop culture.

KABIR
1398 – 1518

Kabir was an Indian poet and spiritual teacher regarded as a saint by Hindu, **Sikh**, and **Sufi** believers. His works and teachings are remarkable in their uncompromising commitment to voicing one's own sincere beliefs, with no fear of criticism and persecution, and no interest in winning fame and followers. Kabir lived in a highly-fragmented society, divided into castes and split between Hinduism, Islam, and other faiths. Yet he didn't hesitate to criticize any religion, or any authority, and didn't care if his poetry offended its readers. He is viewed as an intellectual rebel, a religious reformer, and a source of inspiration for those who stand for freedom of speech.

The Sikhs

Sikhs are followers of Sikhism, a religion and philosophy founded by Guru Nanak Shah in the 15th century in Punjab. The word 'Sikh' comes from Sanskrit 'siksati' – 'to study, to learn.' The Sikh faith focuses on the worship of one God, and states that all people and all religions are equal. As a result of the persecution of non-Muslims by Muslim rulers in India, in the 17th century the Sikh philosophy of tolerance (acceptance of other faiths) was modified. The Sikhs became a warrior community whose law obligates them to defend any believer of any faith against religious persecution. Guru Nanak met Kabir and acknowledged his admiration for Kabir's teaching. The sacred book of the Sikhs, Adi Granth, provides quite a bit of information about Kabir's life.

*"A Sikh warrior"
by Mortimer Ludington Menpes*

Kabir was born in the city of Varanasi in Northern India – a holy city on the sacred Ganges River. His dad was a weaver, likely a Muslim, because **Kabir** is an Arabic word meaning 'big, great." According to a legend, Kabir's parents followed a naming custom popular in Muslim families of that era. Parents would open the Quran, the holy book of Islam, and whatever word first caught their attention would become the child's name. Very little is known about Kabir's life. One of the legends about his birth says that he came from heaven, took the form of a child, and was found and adopted by a Muslim weaver Niru and his wife Nima.

"Whirling Dervishes" by Henri de Montaut, 1870. The Whirling Dervishes are an order of Sufi Muslims who perform a worship ceremony where they turn continuously, with one hand pointing upward and the other pointing toward the ground. It's a form of meditation and prayer.

Sufism

Sufism is a branch of Islam that focuses on the mystical (supernatural) experience of devotion to God. Sufi believers seek to achieve a state of spiritual connection to God through prayer, chanting, ritual dance, and poetry. The word 'Sufi' comes from the Arabic word 'suf' – 'wool.' In the 7th-8th centuries, in Asia and the Middle East, only the wealthy could afford clothes of silk – an expensive import from China. Common people, including Muslim monks and scholars, wore garments of wool.

According to another legend, as a kid, Kabir noticed that the Hindus and the Muslims in his neighborhood despised each other, and started testing their tolerance. When playing with Muslim kids, he would say "Hari, Hari" – repeating one of the holy names of the Hindu god Vishnu – "the one who takes away sins" in Sanskrit. Hearing this, the Muslim kids called him "kafir" (unbeliever). "The only one who is kafir is the one who does evil," responded Kabir. When playing with Hindu kids he painted on his forehead a *tilak* (a mark indicating which subdivision of Hinduism a person belongs to) and wore a *janeo* (the sacred thread worn over the left shoulder by Brahmins, the priestly caste), and repeated the word "Narain" ("the Eternal"– another name of Vishnu). Brahmins saw this and scolded Kabir for wearing priestly symbols. "But this is my faith, too," he responded. "I am a weaver, so I wear a thread."

Growing up, Kabir faced endless accusations from his friends who said he was on the wrong track because he didn't belong to any organized religious group and didn't have a guru – a spiritual teacher. So Kabir decided to become a disciple of Swami Ramananda who lived in Varanasi and was a famous poet and a teacher of Hindu spirituality. Ramananda believed that all people were equal before God. He admitted men of all castes to his school.

Swami

"Swami" means "at one with himself" in Sanskrit – a person who is a master of his thoughts and emotions. It's a title given to Hindu monks.

The problem was, Ramananda accepted very few disciples. Kabir was also afraid that he would be rejected because he had come from a Muslim family. To trick Swami Ramananda into accepting him as a disciple, Kabir came up with this scheme. He decided to find out the *mantra* (sacred prayer words) of Ramananda's school, and use it to convince Ramananda to give him a chance. One day Kabir showed up on the river bank *ghat* where Swami Ramananda often came to bathe. He lay down on the steps that led to the water, just in the right place, and when Ramananda went down the steps, he stumbled on Kabir, and, surprised, exclaimed, "Ram, Ram," repeating the name of the Hindu god Rama. "That's the mantra!" thought Kabir. "The first words that slip off the tongue of a person who repeats these words all the time."

Indian miniature painting "Kabir the weaver"

Next, Kabir told his neighbors that he was about to be accepted as Ramananda's disciple. Both his Hindu and his Muslim friends couldn't believe their ears. To both groups, Kabir was a rebel who didn't think highly of their rituals and customs, and therefore deserved no respect.

Ghats

The City of Varanasi has 88 ghats (steps) leading down to the bank of the Ganges River. Most of these are reserved for Hindu rituals, such as bathing in the Ganges. Two ghats are used for cremations – burning of the dead – since the ancient Hindu belief associates this type of funeral with reaching heaven in the afterlife.

They got together and confronted Ramananda, asking him if, indeed, he had made Kabir one of his disciples. Ramananda didn't know anything about Kabir. When they brought Kabir to meet him, Ramananda asked, "When did I make you my disciple?" "Gurus whisper secret mantras in the ear of their students," answered Kabir, "but you struck me with your foot and loudly called out the name of Rama." Ramananda remembered the kid on the river bank, laughed and hugged Kabir. "Well, you are my disciple now," he said.

Kabir studied sacred books and religious traditions with Swami Ramananda. To make his living he worked as a weaver. Half of the money he made he gave to his mom, the rest he spent on food for the *sadhu* – the Hindu monks he often invited to his house. Kabir cooked for the sadhu, closely following all the rules prescribed for their meals. For example, the food had to be cooked in brand-new pots that had never been used before. Kabir didn't mind following the rules and the rituals, but it annoyed him when rituals were given so much importance that they seemed to replace real faith. One day Kabir was sitting by the Ganges River and listened to Brahmins – members of the priestly caste – preaching that the waters of the Ganges could cleanse a person of their sins. Kabir took his wooden cup, filled it with water from the river, and offered it to one of the Brahmins. The Brahmin refused to drink. To him, Kabir's cup was unclean because Kabir belonged to a low caste. Then Kabir asked him, "If the Ganges water cannot purify my cup, how can I believe that it can wash away my sins?"

To his Hindu critics who accused him of disrespecting the custom of worshiping statues of gods, Kabir responded in poetry:

If by worshiping a stone one can find God,
I shall worship the mountain!
Even the millstones that grind wheat
Are better than the stones you worship.
O human mind,
you make yourself gods and goddesses,
And kill living creatures
to offer them as sacrifices to gods.
But if your gods are real,
why can't they just go and catch these animals
when they are grazing in the fields?

An Indian sadhu – a Hindu monk – talking on his cell phone!

While criticizing religious traditions, Kabir also taught,
Say not that the Hindu or Muslim books are false.
False are the views of those who don't study these books.

Pundit

The word 'pundit' in modern English means 'an expert,' 'an authority' on this or that subject. It comes from the Sanskrit word पण्डित: 'pandita' - 'a learned man, a master.' In India "pandit/pundit" is used to refer to scholars of Hinduism.

Some legends say Kabir married a woman named Loi, and they had a son, Kamal, and a daughter Kamali. Other legends say Kabir wasn't married. Indeed there were two kids, Kamal and Kamali, but they were adopted by Kabir. Kamal had drowned and Kabir found him floating dead down the river. He whispered something into the dead child's ear, and the child came to life and started crying. Kamali was a daughter of Kabir's neighbor. She had also died – of illness – and was brought back to life and adopted by Kabir.

Kabir's daughter appears in another legend. One day Kamali, now 20 years old, was drawing water at a well, when a *pandit* (a Hindu scholar) stopped by and asked her to give him some water. They chatted, but soon the pandit found out that Kamali was a daughter of a common weaver, and got angry. Accepting food or drink from people of low castes was prohibited for a person of his status. Kamali didn't understand why he was upset and called her dad. Kabir knew right away what was going on and said to the pandit, "So you think you were in touch with something impure? What is impurity? You've just drunk water, but in the water you find many dirty things, such as rotten leaves and dead animals... At every step you take, you walk on the dirt which once was living creatures..."

"A Hindu fakir – holy man" and "Weavers working on cashmere shawls," 1863 by William "Crimea" Simpson

"...The clay cups from which you drink are made of earth... You take off your clothes at meals to make sure you don't soil them and wrap yourself in a sheet woven by a common weaver. A fly that visits some filthy places also lands on your food. How can you prevent this? Banish these illusions from your mind, study holy books and pray." The pandit was ashamed of his behavior and asked Kabir to become his teacher. Later he married Kamali.

Criticizing customs and rituals of various religious communities, Kabir got in trouble with both Muslims and Hindus. Finally, Kabir's enemies complained about him to the ruler of the Delhi Sultanate, Sikandar Khan Lodi, accusing Kabir of putting himself above saints and holy books. One of Kabir's poems read,
When the Hindu scholars and the Muslim mullas told me what to do,
I didn't benefit from following their rules, and gave them up.
My heart is pure, I have seen the Lord.
Kabir has searched and searched, all on his own,
And has found God inside himself.

The sultan ordered Kabir to show up at his court, but Kabir said he was busy and arrived to see the sultan only by the evening. When he entered the hall where the sultan sat on his throne, he just stopped and stood in the middle of the hall in silence.
"Why don't you bow before the sultan, you despicable kafir?" the sultan's guards asked him. Kabir replied, "Kafirs are those who can't relate to the suffering of other people. Those who can are saints." The sultan inquired why Kabir hadn't come to the palace in the morning when he was ordered to arrive. "Because I saw something that caught my attention," responded Kabir. "What was that?" "I was watching a caravan of camels passing through a street as narrow as the eye of a needle." "You are such a liar," laughed the sultan. But Kabir replied, "Think of the distance between heaven and earth. Isn't it so vast that it can contain any number of camels and elephants? And all that is in it can be seen through the pupil of the eye which is as small as the eye of a needle." The sultan liked Kabir's answer and was about to let him go, but Kabir's enemies, seething with rage, kept demanding death for Kabir calling him a godless sinner who practiced witchcraft. Kabir tried to explain his teaching to the sultan, but the sultan was tired of noise and arguments. He ordered that Kabir be executed.

The legend about Kabir's execution says that sultan's guards put Kabir in chains and attempted to drown him in a river, but soon after Kabir disappeared under water, they saw him again – this time he looked like a child sitting on a leopard skin floating on the waves!

The guards captured him, locked him in a hut and set the hut on fire... but when the flames died, Kabir reappeared in the form of a beautiful girl. This convinced his executioners that Kabir, indeed, was a master of witchcraft. They seized him again and threw him under the feet of an enraged battle elephant. But Kabir turned into a lion, and the elephant was scared and ran away. At that point the sultan, shocked and amazed, put an end to the "execution," and asked Kabir to forgive him. Kabir responded with a poem,
For him who sows thorns in your path , sow flowers!
Your harvest will be flowers, while his harvest will be pain.

Common people loved Kabir for his simple lifestyle, sense of humor, open-minded approach to religion, and fierce criticism of the rich and the powerful. Most legends about Kabir narrate the stories of his life from the perspective of common people who resented the burden of expensive rituals and rules of "purity" imposed on them by religious authorities. Even the legends about Kabir's death bring forth his idea that faith should be unburdened by superstition and elaborate rituals. In Varanasi they believed that anyone who died in their town, on the sacred banks of the Ganges River, was released from being reborn again, and could go to heaven. But those who died in the town of Maghar, would be reborn again as... donkeys! So when Kabir grew very old, he moved to Maghar. His students begged him to come back to Varanasi, but Kabir refused. He didn't believe that God takes care of people in Varanasi, but not in Maghar. They say that when Kabir died and his body lay in his hut in Maghar covered with cloth, the Hindus and the Muslims stood around it arguing whether to bury Kabir in accordance with the Muslim custom, or to cremate (burn) his body, following the Hindu tradition. Suddenly they heard Kabir's voice that asked them to lift the cloth covering his body. They lifted the cloth and saw that Kabir's body had turned into a heap of flowers! So the Hindus and the Muslims divided the flowers – some were burned, and some were buried.

"Water carriers on the Ganges"
by Edwin Lord Weeks

Here are some of the most famous poetic sayings by Kabir:

What is the use of greatness?
The palm is a tall tree, but nobody sits in its shade and its fruit are out of reach.

In pride there is adversity, in sin there is suffering,
in kindness there is stability, and in forgiveness there is God.

People admire a beautiful painting... Turn away from the painting and think of the painter.

In times of trouble men remember God, but not in times of prosperity.
Should they remember God in times of prosperity, would they ever experience trouble?

The river that flows in you also flows in me.

Do not put the holy books on a high shelf. It'll be hard to reach them.
Do not leave your soul in the hands of a priest. Your soul is your responsibility.

If you are looking for a friend who has no flaws, you'll have no friends.

The clay is molded into a pot, but it is the emptiness inside that makes it useful.

Between the seeker and the object of his search there is a bridge. That bridge is love.

If you want to find God, hang out in the space between your thoughts.

The student is not done with education until he becomes his own teacher.

The mind is everything. What you think, you become.

As long as you live, keep learning how to live.

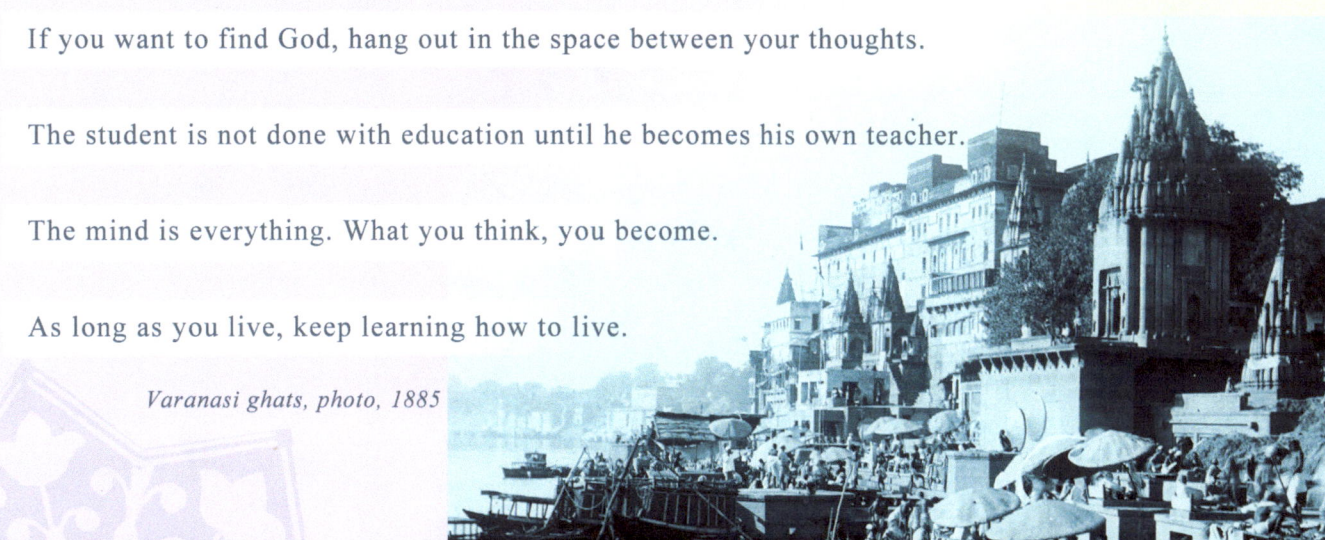

Varanasi ghats, photo, 1885

KRISHNADEVARAYA
1471 – 1529

Krishnadevaraya (Krishna Deva Raya, Raya) was the ruler of the Vijayanagara Empire in South India. He was a brilliant military commander, a patron of the arts, a chess master, and a poet who wrote in two languages – Sanskrit and *Telugu*. His epic poem *Amuktamalyada* is considered a masterpiece of Telugu literature and is read by every student of the Telugu language to this day. Raya upheld the Hindu faith and ancient traditions of South India, and either defeated or prevented invasion attempts by both Muslim sultans from the North, and Portuguese colonizers from the sea.

The Telugu and Tamil languages

Telugu language is spoken by the Telugu people of central and southeastern India. There are over 96 million Telugu speakers! In comparison, there are only about 75 million French and only 65 million Italian-language speakers – worldwide. Telugu belongs to the Dravidian language family. The reign of Krishnadevaraya is considered the "golden age" of Telugu literature.

Tamil is another Dravidian language. It's spoken by the Tamil population of South India and in northern and eastern Sri Lanka. The earliest inscriptions in Tamil date back to the 5th century BC. The famous collection of ancient Tamil poetry – the "Sangam literature" (300 BC – 300 AD) – consists of 2381 poems in Tamil written by 473 poets. Tamil was the language of sailors and traders in ancient India and southeast Asia. Inscriptions in Tamil have been found across Asia and even in Egypt.

"Krishnadeva Raya" by Amar Chitra Katha

Raya's father, Tuluva Narasa Nayaka, was a military commander and a minister in the government of the Vijayanagara king. The king passed away when his two sons were still kids, so Narasa Nayaka, appointed their guardian, ruled the kingdom. After his death in 1505, his eldest son, Raya's half-brother, killed the prince who was the heir to the throne and proclaimed himself king, starting the Tuluva dynasty. Four years later he died, and in 1509 25-year-old Raya was crowned the King of Vijayanagara.

At that time the Kingdom of Vijayanagara was not in good shape. In the East the warlords of Kalinga had seized large chunks of Vijayanagara's lands. From the North the army of Sultan Mahmud of the Bahmani Sultanate of Central India had declared a ***jihad*** (holy war) against Krishnadevaraya and other non-Muslim 'infidels' and had invaded Vijayanagara. So early in his reign Raya waged one war after another torn between multiple battlefields. His first military victory was the defeat of Sultan Mahmud. The sultan was wounded and captured. But as Raya's troops defeated a few more Muslim kingdoms to the North of Vijayanagara, he realized that it would be better to have these lands governed by a local Muslim ruler, who would take orders from Vijayanagara. So he released Sultan Mahmud from captivity and made him governor of his new provinces. The sultan was immensely grateful and gave Krishnadevaraya the title "The Founder of a Muslim Kingdom." This versatility in strategy and practical approach to resolving conflicts became the signature of Raya's style of governance.

The First European colonies in India

After the first successful voyage from Europe to India by Vasco da Gama in 1498, the Portuguese established their first trading posts in India and built a few forts on India's southwest coast. In 1510 they wrestled the city of Goa from the Bijapur Sultanate. The colonial government encouraged Portuguese traders and soldiers to marry local Indian women who converted to Catholicism. This policy created Portuguese-Indian communities and strengthened Portugal's grip on its colonial possessions in India. Goa grew so rich through trade that during the 17th century, in the homes of Goa merchants, everyday-use dishes and cups were made of gold – because silver was considered too cheap! Portuguese colonial rule in Goa lasted until 1961.

The Dutch East India Company started operating in India in 1602. By the mid-17th century it drove the Portuguese out of Ceylon (Sri Lanka) and took over the cinnamon trade there. Next it took away from the Portuguese almost the entire southwest coast of India.

The British East India Company was formed in 1600 to trade with the Spice Islands – the Moluccas islands in present-day Indonesia. Unlike the Portuguese and the Dutch, the British were initially not interested in trading with India or colonizing it. In 1607 an English vessel sailing to the Spice Islands was driven off course by a storm and came to the port of Surat, in Gujarat, India. The East India Company requested permission to open a trading post in Surat, and in 1612 Mughal Emperor Jahangir granted it. When English King Charles II married a Portuguese princess, Catherine of Braganza, in 1662, he received the Portuguese colonial possessions in Bombay as part of her **dowry** (dowry = property or money given as a contribution to the welfare of the new family). Bombay (now Mumbai) became the headquarters of British colonial expansion on the West coast of India, while Madras (now Chennai) played the same role on its East coast.

The French East India Company was founded in 1664. 10 years later it acquired Pondicherry from the Sultan of Bijapur and in 1692 it received permission from the Mughal governor of Bengal to establish a trading post in the port of Chandernagore. Pondicherry and Chandernagore remained under French control until 1954.

Ruins of the Raichur Fort

The strength of the Indian armies of that era depended entirely on cavalry. Krishnadevaraya believed that the best horses were the Arab and Persian horses which the Portuguese brought to their trading posts in Goa. So he made friends with some Portuguese colonists and persuaded them to sell to him all the horses they had, as well as guns. In 1520 the Portuguese helped Raya to conquer a fort in the city of Raichur in the Bahmani Sultanate. In return the Portuguese hoped to get permission to open trade in the growing Vijayanagara Empire. Raya negotiated with the Portuguese with great caution. He knew that at the first opportunity they would try to seize his land. Once Raya pushed away the invaders, he expanded his kingdom into a vast empire stretching across the whole of South India.

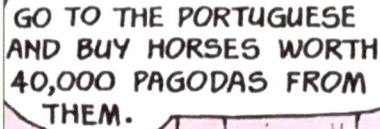

From "Krishnadeva Raya" by Amar Chitra Katha

Krishnadevaraya had two wives – one of them was a princess, and the other – a famous court dancer. He had 3 kids. In 1514 he visited a temple in the town of Tirupati with his queens. In honor of this visit copper statues of the emperor and his wives, praying, were set up in the temple. They can be seen today in the Tirupati museum.

In his capital, Raya constructed a special building for cultural activities. Here poets recited their works – in Sanskrit, Telugu, Tamil, and other Indian languages, and theater collectives staged plays, some of which were written by Raya himself. Eight of the court poets were jointly given the title "Mighty like the Eight Elephants" – an echo of an Indian myth saying that the earth rests on the backs of eight elephants.

One of the famous Telugu poets at Raya's court, Allasani Peddana, described in his poems the respect with which Krishnadevaraya treated him. When the poet dedicated one of his works to the king, Raya lifted and carried Allasani Peddana's palanquin along with his servants. On another occasion, when Raya spotted the poet in the street, he stopped his elephant and helped Allasani Peddana up to sit next to him on the elephant's back.

For his support of the arts, Raya was praised as "the bright sun at dawn, shining with the radiance of the nine gems."

A water tank called "The Dancing Girls' Pool" in Krishnadevaraya's capital, Hampi

While Raya's empire flourished, the king's family life was shaken by a tragedy. For many years the emperor didn't have a son, an heir to his throne. Finally, in 1518, his princess wife, Tirumala Devi, gave birth to a boy. To make sure that his son's claim to the crown would never be disputed, Raya stepped down from his throne and proclaimed his son – still a little kid – the King of Vijayanagara. From now on Raya himself was just his son's Prime Minister. Sadly, only a few months later the boy got sick and died. Tormented by grief, Krishnadevaraya suspected his son was poisoned. Some of the nobles at his court used this opportunity to settle scores with their enemies, and blamed Timma Dandanayaka, the son of Raya's most trusted minister. The king believed this. After all, his own brother, a son of a royal minister, had murdered the crown prince of Vijayanagara and started his own dynasty. Raya locked Timma Dandanayaka in jail, but 3 years later Timma escaped and started a rebellion in the remote provinces of Raya's empire. The rebellion was suppressed, Timma, his father and brother were blinded and jailed. These events undermined the image of Krishnadevaraya as the all-powerful invincible ruler. Rebels in the imperial provinces and the Muslim kings in the North of the empire waited for a chance to strike and tear the Vijayanagara Empire apart. Raya died from sickness in 1529 leaving the crown to his half-brother. Right away the enemies of the empire invaded Vijayanagara from every direction. The armies of the sultans from the North defeated Vijayanagara in 1565, destroying and plundering its cities.

Right: The famous Stone Chariot at the Vitthala Temple in Hampi, the capital of the Vijayanagara Empire. It was cut from one rock, and its wheels could turn!
Above: Matanga Hill temple, Hampi

Guru Nanak
1469 – 1539

Guru Nanak was the founder and the first guru of the Sikh faith. His spiritual teaching promoted religious and social harmony. Guru Nanak was born in the village of Talwandi near Lahore in Punjab, present-day Pakistan. His dad, a Hindu merchant whose name was Mehta Kalu, tried to train him in different professions, but Nanak was more interested in studying sacred texts and discussing philosophical and religious issues with monks in the forests around his village. Very early he came to the conclusion that "There are no Hindus, and no Muslims..." "Rituals are useless..." "Rather than temples, God prefers a pure heart." In other words, no matter what religion people follow and what rituals they perform, in the eyes of God they are all equal – as long as they reject selfishness and evil.

"Guru Nanak"
a vintage postcard

When Nanak turned 10, his dad arranged for him the janeu ceremony. Nanak was to receive the janeu, a cotton thread that symbolizes belonging to the Brahmin, Kshatriya, or Vaishya castes. Hindu men wear the janeu over the left shoulder, across the body. When a priest offered Nanak the janeu, Nanak refused to accept it. The priest insisted: "Unless you wear this thread, you'll be a man with no religion." But Nanak objected: "Men steal, cheat, abuse one another... but they wear a cotton thread that a Brahmin twisted for them... and when they die, the thread is just tossed away." He later summed up his thoughts in these poetic words:

Out of the cotton of compassion,
Spin the thread of happiness,
Tie the knot of self-control,
Give it the twist of virtues.
Make such a sacred thread,
For your inner self.
Such a thread will not break,
Nor get soiled, burnt, or lost...

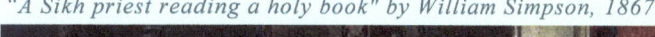
"A Sikh priest reading a holy book" by William Simpson, 1867

Kalu tried to get his son interested in business. He gave him some money and asked him to purchase salt in one village and sell it in another village to make some profit. But on the way to purchase salt, Nanak ran into some traveling monks who hadn't eaten for three days. He gave his dad's money to the monks. At home, when Kalu asked him how much profit he had made, Nanak responded, "I made profit that is eternal – by feeding the poor."

A Langar

*Guru Nanak's generosity in feeding the poor is reflected in the Sikh **Langar** tradition. A langar is a community kitchen run by Sikh volunteers who cook and serve meals free of charge to anyone in need, no matter their religion or ethnicity. The meals are usually lacto-vegetarian. People eat sitting on the floor of a communal room.*

"Langar" – a vintage print

Kalu was extremely upset but didn't give up yet. Nanak was already around 18, and Kalu hoped that if Nanak got married and had a family, he would be more interested in making money. So he found a bride for his son and Nanak got married. But soon after his wedding Nanak met a traveling holy man who had no money for food or shelter and gave him the only valuable things he happened to have with him – a brass jug and his gold wedding ring. Kalu's patience was over, and he kicked Nanak out of his house. Fortunately, Nanak's brother-in-law was a manager of granaries (grain storehouses) of the Delhi Sultanate's Lahore governor whose office was in Sultanpur. He offered Nanak a job. Nanak moved to Sultanpur, and a year later had enough money to buy a house for himself and his wife Mata Sulakhani. Kalu was beyond happy!

Nanak liked his job because the governor allowed him to give away some grain to the poor. However, Nanak felt the amount reserved for charity was not enough. A lot of people still starved. So Nanak cut his own salary to the point where he was eating only dry bread, giving away as much to the poor as he could. Nanak's caring and compassionate attitude to the poor made him popular. Envious of his success, some government officials complained that he had been wasting too much grain "on beggars," but failed to prove their accusations. Guru Nanak worked as the granary manager for 12 years. He and his wife had 2 sons. And then came a day when Nanak suddenly disappeared and was missing for three days. What happened? Sikh believers and scholars say Guru Nanak spent these days in meditation and prayer, and received a revelation, a message from God. It was the **Mul Mantar**, the foundation of the Sikh faith, that became the first words of the Sikh holy book Guru Granth Sahib:

There is one God,
Eternal Truth is His Name,
The Creator of all things,
He has no fear and no hate,
timeless, not born, but eternal,
known by the grace of the Guru.

When Guru Nanak returned home and started preaching, his friends and family must have been in shock. In Nanak's own words, "When man loves the Lord, when he considers himself worthless, and views the rest of the world as good, people call him mad." But Nanak wasn't disheartened. He called on Hindus and Muslims to realize that their faith should unite them rather than split them apart. "Put on armor," he taught, "that will harm no one. Let your chainmail coat be your understanding, and turn your enemies into friends. Fight with courage, but with no weapon, except the word of God."

Just like Kabir, Guru Nanak angered both Hindu and Muslim authorities. One day a mullah (a Muslim scholar) was offended when he saw Guru Nanak lying on the ground because his feet seemed to point in the direction of the holy Muslim city of Mecca. "How dare you, infidel, turn your feet toward the house of God?" exclaimed the mullah. "Well, why won't you turn them in a direction where the house of God is not," responded Nanak. Nanak's enemies kept attacking him and soon the Delhi Sultanate governor demanded to know what Nanak meant by saying "there are no Hindus, and no Muslims." "Being a Muslim is hard," answered Nanak. "You should joyfully obey the will of God, worship the Creator and give up any self interest...

When you are kind to all men, then you can be called a Muslim... Let compassion be your mosque, let faith be your prayer mat, let honesty be your Quran."

Nanak traveled across India and South Asia and beyond– to Tibet and Arabia preaching the principles of his faith – charity, compassion, and tolerance. He became so famous, people told stories of miracles he had performed. Sikh scholars vary in their interpretations of Guru Nanak's teaching. Some believe that he was a prophet and his teaching is a direct revelation (message) from God. Others say that Nanak was not a prophet, but was rather a religious reformer who taught people to discard rituals and religious institutions that split them into different faiths, and to seek direct communication with God...who would unite them.

Vintage and modern pictures of the Sikh Golden Temple in Amritsar

AKBAR THE GREAT
1542 – 1605

Emperor Akbar

By the early 16th century the Sultanate of Delhi was in decline. Meanwhile, in the North, in Central Asia, a new force was rising – Babur, a descendant of the great Mongol conquerors Genghis Khan and Timur (Tamerlane). Babur became the ruler of a kingdom in the Fergana Valley (present-day Uzbekistan) when he was 12 years old. Local Uzbek warlords didn't take him seriously and rebelled. But Babur raised an army of loyal supporters and at 14 he conquered Samarkand, the greatest city on the Silk Road in Central Asia. However, Babur's campaign didn't go smoothly. He conquered Samarkand, but he lost Fergana. He tried to recapture Fergana, and lost Samarkand! Finally the Uzbek princes kicked him out of Uzbekistan, and Babur, now 21, led his army to Kabul in Afghanistan. He conquered Kabul, and, with the help of the Persians, brought Samarkand back under his rule... only to lose it again, a third time! That's when Babur turned his gaze to the weakened Delhi Sultanate. Its provinces of Oudh, Behar, and Punjab revolted against the Sultan of Delhi and sent messengers to Kabul asking Babur to come and take over. With the help of the Persian and Ottoman rulers, Babur defeated the Sultan of Delhi in 1526 and founded the **Mughal Empire**. Babur was a poet and had a passion for gardening. Many of his poems, written in Turki, his native Turkic language, became folk songs.

The Mughal Empire lasted more than 300 years, until 1857, when the British **East India Company** crushed the Indian Rebellion – a revolt against British colonial rule. The 20th and the last Mughal emperor, Bahadur Shah Zafar, who at that point ruled only the walled city of Delhi, participated in the rebellion, and was forced by the British off the throne and into exile.

Akbar the Great was the grandson of Babur and the third emperor of the Mughal Empire in India. Along with growing his empire, his greatest achievement was a policy of tolerance that won him the loyalty of his non-Muslim subjects. During Akbar's reign, talented men of all religions were promoted to high positions in the government and the military. Trade and commerce tripled in volume, and cultural diversity was welcome across the empire.

Mogul

*The English word **mogul** – "a powerful person," comes from 'mughal'! 'Mughal' was a Persian term for 'Mongol.' Even though most of the Mughal rulers in India were of Turkic, not Mongolian origin, 'mughal' was used to refer to all Central Asians.*

After Babur's death in 1530, his son Humayun became king, but he faced a rebellion and fled to Sindh, in present-day Pakistan, where a local Hindu ruler offered him refuge. Over there Humayun married Hamida Banu Begum, daughter of his younger brother's teacher, and they had a baby – the future Emperor Akbar. Hamida Banu Begum's family was Persian (Iranian), and she helped Humayun to create a lasting alliance with Iran. Akbar's education focused on hunting and fighting skills. He wasn't taught to read or to write. But his mom collected books and read to him every night. Modern scholars suggest Akbar could have been dyslexic, because even as a grownup he had someone read to him every day, but never read himself.

"The great Mughal and his court returning from the Great Mosque in Delhi" by Edwin Lord Weeks

When Akbar was 9 years old, his father Humayun appointed him to be the governor of Ghazni, one of the provinces of Afghanistan, and the commander of the Ghazni army. When Akbar turned 12, his dad reconquered Delhi. However, only a few months later he fell down the steps of his library at the royal fortress in Delhi and died. Royal advisors concealed his death until Akbar, now 13 years-old, and still fighting the Delhi rebels, was crowned sultan. The coronation followed the Mongol tradition. Akbar received his father's sword, a bejeweled pin with a crane's feather was attached to his turban, and he was led to his throne – a pile of cushions covered with goat skins. The servants held yak tails and the royal umbrella over Akbar's head. The great silver kettle drum sounded outside, and heralds proclaimed that from that day on all Mughal coins would be stamped with the new emperor's name.

For a few years Akbar ruled the empire with the help of his guardian, Mughal military commander Bairam Khan. Akbar's relationship with his guardian was tense at times. When Akbar was 14, his troops defeated Hemu, an Indian king who resisted the Mughal invasion. Hemu was wounded by an arrow and brought to the Mughal camp unconscious. Bairam Khan told Akbar to behead Hemu so that Akbar could claim the title of 'Ghazi' – the Slayer of the Infidels. But cutting the head off an enemy who was unconscious and a prisoner of war felt wrong, so Akbar refused. Bairam Khan, however, pressed him to obey, and finally Akbar picked up his scimitar (a sword with a curved blade) and hit Hemu, who was already likely dead, on the neck. Hemu's head was sent to Kabul as a trophy. This episode cast a shadow on Akbar's relationship with Bairam Khan.

Khan

Khan *was a royal title in Turkic kingdoms. In Turkic languages 'khan' means 'lord, prince.' The female form of 'khan' is 'khanum.'*

Bairam Khan was not the only trusted advisor to the young Mughal emperor. There was yet another "power behind the throne" – Akbar's nanny, Maham Anga, who had helped raise Akbar. When he was a little kid, she served as his foster mother while his parents traveled to Iran to secure Persian military help. Akbar had a tremendous respect for Maham Anga. He called her 'mother,' kissed her hands when greeting her, and when she entered the room, he always offered her his own seat. Akbar listened to Maham Anga's advice, and over the years she became the manager of the royal household and the most powerful person at his court. All the palace ceremonies, receptions, festivals, parties and everyday meals were designed and run by Maham Anga.

"Bairam Khan" – a Mughal painting

Her loyalty, however, was divided between Akbar and her own son, Adham Khan, treated by Akbar as his own brother. Adham Khan was a military commander in the Mughal army, but Bairam Khan was not impressed with him and didn't promote him to higher ranks. Maham Anga hoped Akbar would help her son, but Bairam Khan never let Akbar out of his sight, and it was practically impossible to talk to him without Bairam Khan listening in. In 1560 Maham Anga told Akbar that his mom was sick – it was a lie! Akbar rushed to see her in India, leaving Bairam Khan back in Afghanistan. Once Akbar was away from Bairan Khan, Maham Anga convinced him it was time to rule on his own – he was almost 18! Bairam Khan had to go!

Needless to say, Bairam Khan didn't want to let go of the enormous power he had. One day, extremely annoyed, he made a blunder by criticizing some decisions Akbar made in front of the entire royal court. Infuriated, Akbar dismissed him as his royal advisor and ordered him to leave on Hajj (Muslim pilgrimage) to Mecca. While in Punjab, on his way to Mecca, Bairam Khan changed his mind and started gathering troops to revolt against Akbar. Akbar found out and sent an army that quickly defeated and captured Bairam Khan. Bairam Khan appeared before the emperor dressed as a beggar, bare-footed, his turban folded around his neck. He fell face down before the throne and, crying, touched the carpet with his forehead. Akbar forgave his former guardian and offered him a choice – to stay at his court like nothing happened, or to continue his pilgrimage to Mecca. Bairam Khan chose to leave. As he traveled across Afghanistan, he was recognized by a local prince whose father had perished fighting against the Mughal army led by Bairam Khan. The prince organized an ambush and Bairam Khan was murdered. Maham Anga now became Akbar's most trusted advisor. Historians of the Mughal Empire nicknamed Maham Anga and also Akbar's mom, Hamida Banu Begum, the 'petticoat (skirt) government' – so strong was their influence on Akbar.

Akbar started expanding the Mughal Empire with the Malwa Sultanate in Central India then ruled by Afghan Sultan Baz Bahadur. One of the commanders who led the Mughal army on this campaign was Adham Khan. At first the campaign was very successful, but there were a couple things that bothered Akbar. Adham Khan seized and kept all the treasures left by Baz Bahadur as he fled his capital. Adham neither offered them to Akbar, nor divided them with other commanders. Also, as the Afghan troops surrendered, Adham Khan ordered them all to be slaughtered to the last man. And not only the soldiers – his army also massacred the wives and kids of the Afghans who defended the Malwa capital, Mandu, and even Afghan Muslim scholars who walked out of mosques with holy books in their hands. Akbar's contemporary, Mughal historian and poet Abd al-Qadir Badayuni, who witnessed the massacre, wrote, "On the day of the victory, the two commanders had the captives brought before them, and group after group they were put to death, so that their blood flowed like river upon river." This was a common practice in Central Asia where Mughals came from, but in India such atrocities toward civilians were rare. Akbar felt that Adam Khan's behavior disgraced him. Plus, there was another disturbing rumor circulating at the Delhi court. It was about Adham Khan's role in the death of Baz Bahadur's queen, the Hindu beauty and poetess Roopmati.

Roopmati was a common village girl with a stunningly-beautiful voice. She wrote and sang her own poetry. Baz Bahadur, who was a great lover of music, heard her singing in the fields as she guarded her family's sheep and proposed to her. She agreed to follow him to his capital, Mandu, on the condition that she would have windows overlooking the river by which she had grown up – Narmada. Baz Bahadur built for her a palace on the bank of the river. Roopmati was a living legend in Malwa and well beyond.

Left: "Roopmati and Baz Bahadur" – a Mughal painting
Below: "Baz Bahadur asks Roopmati to be his queen" by M.V. Dhurandhar

When Adham Khan's army stormed the royal palace in Mandu, he met Roopmati and was stunned by her beauty and by the dignity with which she faced him. He suggested that she dump Baz Bahadur, who had been defeated and fled, and become his, Adham Khan's girlfriend. Roopmati responded that "it did not become the glory of the conqueror" to seek to disgrace the conquered in this way. "One day heaven may bring down shame on the head of the conqueror," she said. That night Roopmati dressed as a flower seller and escaped from the palace to her family in the countryside. Adham Khan sent his men to chase her. They killed her parents and brothers, and finally captured Roopmati. Unable to escape again, Roopmati poisoned herself and died. This story shocked the Mughal court in Delhi. Adham Khan's victory lost its glory. Akbar rushed to Malwa to tell Adham Khan face to face that he was fired. But the worst was still ahead!

When Akbar and Adham Khan returned to Delhi, Baz Bahadur invaded Malwa with some new allies, and took back Mandu. The Mughal army sent to defeat him was destroyed. The relationship between Adham Khan and Akbar was now disastrous. It was only a matter of time until it would blow up.

Ruins of Baz Bahadur's palace and Roopmati's pavilion (below); Roopmati and Baz Bahadur from the 1931 Bollywood film "Rani Roopmati" ("Queen Roopmati")

In 1561 Akbar appointed a new prime minister, Ataga Khan. Ataga Khan was one of his generals and his personal friend. Maham Anga, however, hated him. One morning Ataga Khan was sitting in the royal audience hall (a hall where the emperor received visitors), and waited for Akbar who was still asleep. Suddenly, in came Adham Khan and a couple of his officers, and murdered Ataga Khan. They tried to escape, but Akbar, awakened by the noise, rushed into the audience hall and caught Adham. Shocked at Ataga Khan murder, Akbar lost it. He knocked Adham out with his fist and ordered his guards to throw him off a second-floor terrace into the palace courtyard. The guards fulfilled his order. Akbar ran downstairs to see the "result": Adham was badly wounded but still alive. So Akbar told the guards to grab Adham, drag him up to the terrace again and toss him down into the courtyard the second time. After Adham Khan died, Akbar went to Maham Anga and told her what happened. She listened to the news in silence and then responded, "Your Majesty has done well."

40 days after she buried her son, Maham Anga passed away from grief. Akbar built a beautiful mausoleum (tomb) for Maham Anga and Adham Khan, ending this dramatic chapter of his youth. Akbar was 20, with 40 years on the throne of the biggest empire in the history of India still ahead of him. Baz Bahadur was eventually defeated, his kingdom becoming a part of the Mughal Empire. For nearly 10 years he lived at the courts of various enemies of Akbar, but in 1570 he traveled to Delhi, reconciled with Akbar, and accepted Akbar's offer to be a general in his army.

"Death of Adham Khan" – a Mughal painting; a Mughal ring cut from a solid emerald, 16th century

Roopmati

In 1926 a collection of Roopmati's poems was first translated into English and published in London under the title "The Lady of the Lotus: Rupmati, Queen of Mandu, A Strange Tale of Faithfulness." Here are 2 poems by Roopmati.

Not time, nor space can ruin love.
It does not die when lovers part.
A rock sunk deep beneath a lake
Keeps star fire in its heart.

In ocean depths I often dove,
Yet won no pearl from out the sea.
The ocean I do not blame,
I blame only fate and me.

Akbar

Names **Kabir** and **Akbar** come from the Arabic root KBR – 'big.' In Arabic, "Kabir" (كبير) is an adjective – "great, big." "Akbar" (أكبر) can be a comparative degree of this adjective – "greater," or its superlative degree – "the greatest." The word "akbar" appears in **Takbir**, the Arabic phrase **Allahu Akbar** (الله أكبر) – "God is the greatest" – used in Muslim prayers and the call to prayer. "Takbir" also comes from the root KBR. It's a verb meaning "to magnify, proclaim greatness" – proclaiming the greatness of God.

The Rajputs

The term **Rajput** refers to warrior clans that formed in the early Middle Ages in North India. The word 'Rajput' comes from the Sanskrit 'rajaputra' – 'son of a king.' It's likely that originally people became 'Rajputs' based on their occupation and social status (mercenary fighters and land owners), but eventually membership in the Rajput clans became hereditary.

Throughout his reign, almost non-stop, Akbar fought wars of conquest and military campaigns against the rebels inside the empire. He won most of his battles, but preferred not to punish or replace the defeated princes and rebel leaders. Once they recognized his superiority, he would just let them rule their lands as part of the Mughal Empire. For example, Uzbek warlords revolted three times between 1564 and 1566. Every time, after his troops put out the uprisings, Akbar forgave their leaders, except for the third time. During the conquest of the Garha Kingdom in North India, Mughal general Asaf Khan seized 1000 elephants and huge quantities of gold from the Garha treasury, but he kept most of the treasures and sent only 200 elephants to Akbar. When Akbar confronted him about it, Asaf Khan fled to the Uzbek warlords and joined their revolt. The Mughal forces defeated him and Asaf Khan begged Akbar's forgiveness. Akbar – with his usual generosity – pardoned him and returned him to his general's position. One notorious instance when Akbar displayed utter ruthlessness was when he conquered Rajput lands in North-Western India. The Rajput kingdom of Mewar had never before been subdued by Islamic rulers, and was viewed as the stronghold of the Hindu faith and tradition. Its king descended from Rajput fighters who defeated Babur. Mewar soldiers were the best-trained among the Rajputs. When Akbar took the fortress-capital of Mewar after months of siege, he ordered the slaughter of not only its defenders, but also 30 thousand women and kids sheltering in the fortress. Then he built special towers all across the Rajput lands and had the heads of the Mewar Rajputs nailed to them to terrify everyone into submission.

While ruthless to Hindu rebels, Akbar treated the Hindus who accepted his rule with fairness and respect. He banned the *Jazia* – a tax imposed on non-Muslims that forced poorer Hindus who couldn't afford it, to convert to Islam. Hindus were given high offices in his government.

Many of Akbar's top military commanders were Hindus. When Akbar sent his troops to put down a rebellion in Afghanistan, his Hindu officers refused to cross the Indus River because of the **Kala Pani** "curse." Kala Pani ("black water" or "sea water") was a traditional Hindu belief that crossing the seas to travel to foreign lands constituted a violation of divine laws and made the traveler impure, destroying his social status. Many Hindus of the Mughal era believed that crossing the Indus River in the North East of India also fell under the Kala Pani curse.
To convince his Hindu officers to cross the river, Akbar gave them 8 months of pay in advance!

Mariam-uz-Zamani

Mariam-uz-Zamani was born a Rajput princess, daughter of Raja Bihari Mal, ruler of the Kingdom of Amber. The raja suggested that Akbar marry his daughter so that the Rajput royalty could be bound to the Mughals by family ties. Mariam's Hindu name was Harkha Bai (also rendered as Jodha Bai). She became the third and favorite wife of Akbar, and was given the title Mariam-uz-Zamani (Mother for all Ages) when her son, Prince Salim, the future emperor Jahangir, was born. Like his dad, Salim had a deep respect for his mother throughout his life. He greeted her by going down on his knees and touching her feet. He carried her palanquin along with her servants. It's likely that Mariam never abandoned her Hindu faith. Akbar built for her the Nilkanth Temple dedicated to Shiva in the ancient town of Mandu and ordered everyone at his court to be standing when Mariam held the **Homa***. Homa is a fire ritual when offerings – such as seeds or grains – are burned as a form of prayer. Akbar also started celebrating the Hindu* **Diwali** *festival and would drink only water that had been brought to him from the Ganges River! Even when he traveled far from the Ganges, his caravan carried the Ganges water in sealed jars for him to drink. Akbar stopped eating beef, since cows are sacred animals in Hinduism, and ordered every nobleman to give Mariam a jewel every year for the New Year's celebration. It's possible that it was marriage to Mariam that prompted Akbar to adopt the attitude of tolerance toward other religions. Mariam and Akbar had 10 kids.*

Mariam was an entrepreneur. She set up a shipping business in Lahore. The ships she owned were used to import silk and spices, and also to take Muslim pilgrims to Arabia. Akbar invested money in her trading business, but it was run entirely by Mariam. After Akbar's death, her largest ship, 'Rahimi,' was seized and robbed by the Portuguese Navy. In response, Mariam's son, Emperor Jahangir, captured the town of Daman in the Portuguese colony of Goa and jailed all its Portuguese residents.

Right: Mughal paintings of Mariam-uz-Zamani and Prince Salim

Diwali

Diwali is a 5-day Hindu festival of lights symbolizing the victory of good over evil. It is celebrated in the fall, in October-November. 'Diwali' comes from the Sanskrit 'dīpāvali' – lights in a row. During this festival people decorate their homes, offices, and temples with oil lamps called **diyas** and floor designs, **rangolis**. A rangoli is a circular pattern created on the floor with easy-to-find materials, such as colored rocks, sand, charcoal, rice, spices, or flower petals.

When home from the battlefronts, Akbar presided over a spectacular court and cultivated art and education in the many languages of his realm. He founded a system of schools for both Muslims and Hindus, and a library for women. His own library contained 24 thousand books in Sanskrit, Urdu, Persian, Greek, Latin, Arabic, and Kashmiri. Akbar welcomed Muslim, Hindu, Sikh, Jain, and other scholars at his court and encouraged them to hold weekly lectures and debates on religious topics. He also invited Catholic missionaries from the Portuguese colony of Goa on the Western coast of India to join these discussions and explain their Christian faith to his court. These religious gatherings were held in a special building – the Ibadat Khana (the House of Worship).

Akbar's relationship with his son and the heir to the Mughal throne, Salim, was strained. Salim – he future Emperor Jahangir – seemed to always balance on the brink of rebellion. He was a drug user, addicted to opium (a drug made from poppy plants), and an alcoholic, even though Islam prohibits drinking alcohol. His parties and crazy behavior when drunk caused endless scandals at Akbar's court. But Salim was Akbar's only surviving son, and Akbar shared power with him, giving him provinces to rule and wars to win. Akbar also believed that disciplining or punishing his son was incompatible with Salim's royal status and destiny as the future ruler of the empire. The father and the son disagreed on a lot of things. While Akbar viewed himself as a protector of all religions, Salim had no tolerance for non-Muslims. Salim was an accomplished writer. Here is how he described a conversation he had with his dad when Akbar prohibited him from raiding and plundering a Hindu temple in Varanasi:

"Having on one occasion asked my father why he had forbidden anyone to destroy these nests of idol-worshiping [Hindu temples], his reply was in the following terms: 'My dear child, I consider myself a powerful monarch, the shadow of God upon Earth. I have seen that God gives the blessings of His gracious providence to all His creatures without distinction. If I were to withhold my compassion from any people God gave me to rule over, I would betray the trust extended to me in my high position. With all of the human race, with all God's creatures, I am at peace. Why then should I permit myself to be the cause of aggression to anyone? Besides, are not five out of six men [in India] either Hindus or folk of other religions? So if I follow your ideas, am I supposed to put them all to death? I have reflected on this, and believe the only wise thing to do is to leave these men alone. Also, don't forget that the class of people we are talking about are usefully engaged in either pursuit of science, or the arts, or other improvements for the benefit of mankind.'"

A Mughal book illustration: Adham Khan kisses the foot of Akbar; Next page: Emperor Jahangir

Mughal Painting

Mughal painting is a style of art that developed at the court of Mughal emperors. It borrowed its technique and look from Persian manuscript illustrations. Mughal paintings illustrated historical chronicles, works of literature, and reports of events at the court and in the emperor's family. Emperor Akbar had an album of portraits depicting his court officials, commanders, and governors. In the portraits officials held objects representing their work and status. The album helped the emperor to remember who he had appointed for various positions.

Islamic tradition prohibits depicting human form in art. Typically, art and design in Muslim countries stay away from portraying people. Instead, they employ such elements as geometric patterns, calligraphy (stylized writing), and motifs from nature. However, the secular (non-religious) art of the Persian and Mughal empires broke with this Islamic tradition and focused on portraits and scenes of court and military life.

Sadly, none of Akbar's personal discipline and tolerance rubbed off on Salim. Salim took advantage of his dad's compassionate parenting philosophy and simply ignored him. To awaken the spirit of an imperial ruler in Salim, Akbar ordered him to confront yet another Rajput rebellion. But Salim preferred the luxury of his province-governor's palace to being in a saddle on a military march. In his writings he recalled with horror accompanying his father on a military campaign in Kashmir and feeling so hungry that he was thrilled to eat lamb chops roasted on fire – even without any spices or side dishes!!! Salim valued comfort above all. Next came opium, alcohol, and flattery from his courtiers.

One time Akbar tried to save Salim from his addictions by locking him up in his palace with no opium or alcohol allowed. Suffering from alcohol and drug withdrawal (physical pain and depression experienced by drug addicts in the absence of drugs), Salim humiliated himself by getting down on his knees to beg his guards for wine. He behaved even more crazily than when he was drunk. Akbar was afraid that Salim would lose his mind and kill himself, and called a doctor asking him to figure out the minimum alcohol that Salim could drink every day without suffering the withdrawal. But Salim's mom, Mariam-uz-Zamani, interfered and made her husband let Salim go. Sadly, many years later, it was indeed the drug addiction that eroded the health of Emperor Jahangir – and eventually killed him.

Many of Salim's friends couldn't wait for his old dad to be gone. As Salim listened to their flattery, he started thinking that the throne should pass to him without the need to wait for his dad to die. Instead of fighting fearless Rajputs he figured he could seize one of his father's provinces – like Punjab – and rule it as a king. Or maybe he could wait for his father's army to be away from his capital, Agra, and seize the city with its untold treasures and armories... Sure enough, when Akbar left on a military campaign against a rebellious province, Salim assembled some forces, marched to Agra, and demanded that the city surrender. But the governor of Agra – an excellent diplomat – pretended he didn't understand what Salim had in mind.

He ordered the city garrison to ignore Salim and his army. Confused, Salim retreated and headed to Allahabad (the Mughal name of today's Prayagraj). Terrified of the inevitable catastrophe, one of his military commanders, Man Singh, got in touch with Akbar and shared with him Salim's plans. Akbar's mom, Hamida Banu Begum, also learned about Salim's intentions. When her grandson was passing close to her residence on his way to Allahabad, she left home and chased him, hoping to talk him out of revolt. But Salim changed his route to avoid her.

In Allahabad, Salim plundered the city treasury. At that point Akbar called him to show up at the imperial court and explain himself. His message was openly threatening. Man Singh was afraid that rebels across the empire would hear of Salim's revolt and join him. He also knew that Akbar could not afford to lose his only son and the heir to his throne. So Man Singh came up with an ingenious plan to allow Salim back out of his scheme and to hide the fact that he had revolted. He suggested that Akbar order Salim to join other Mughal troops in suppressing rebels in the East. That would explain his marching around at the head of his army. Akbar followed his advice, and the storm blew over. Salim changed his mind about rebelling. Man Singh was given the highest military rank and a rich reward for his loyalty. Years later, writing about his life, Emperor Jahangir summed up his own version of these events in one sentence: "Certain vagabonds caused a misunderstanding between me and my father."

In his last years Akbar fell into the habit of taking opium and spent most of his time alone, avoiding his court. He died of dysentery, a disease caused by food contamination. It was very common. Dysentery bacteria were always breeding in the horse and cattle manure in the streets and in the fields, and flies carried the infection to the kitchens and dinner tables of both peasants and kings.

The Taj Mahal

The Taj Mahal is a masterpiece of Mughal architecture constructed in 1631 in Agra by Akbar's grandson Emperor Shah Jahan as the tomb of his queen, Mumtaz Mahal. It is built of white marble, carved and decorated with semi-precious stones. "Taj Mahal" means "Crown of the Palace" in Urdu.

SHIVAJI
1630 – 1680

Indian movie star Chandrakant Jagirdar as Shivaji in the 1952 Bollywood film "Chhatrapati Shivaji"

By the mid-17th century the Mughal Empire started losing its grip on the **Deccan** ("the South") – central-southern India. The **Marathas**, Hindu clans who lived in the mountains of the Western Deccan, took advantage of this, and formed their own independent Maratha Kingdom under the leadership of a fearless warlord, Shivaji. Eventually Shivaji's kingdom grew into a vast and powerful Maratha Confederacy, or Maratha Empire. In India, Shivaji is viewed as a national hero, an independence fighter. There are many monuments to Shivaji. In Mumbai, the biggest airport and the railway station are named after him. The events of Shivaji's life read like the plot of a thriller movie. Indeed, he is a hero of dozens of movies, novels, and comic books. In the Indian state of Maharashtra, every year during the festival of Diwali, kids build mud-and-rock models of forts populated with toy soldiers and an action figure of... King Shivaji.

Shivaji

Shivaji was named after Hindu goddess Shivai, revered in Maratha lands. 'Ji' in his name is a suffix that appeared in many Maratha names. It comes from Hindi 'Ji' as a title of respect, similar to 'lord,' 'sir.' Today 'ji' is often added to a name to show respect while addressing a person.

Shivaji was born to the family of a military commander who served the Sultan of Bijapur, one of the Muslim kingdoms in the Deccan, while also ruling his own small princedom, Pune. On his dad's side Shivaji was a descendant of the Rajput royal family of Mewar – the kingdom ravaged by Akbar in 1567. Shivaji's father, Shahaji, had at some point served in the Mughal army, but rebelled. To keep Shahaji in Deccan and away from the Mughal heartland, the Mughal government made a deal with the Sultan of Bijapur. He would accept Shahaji into his service, but on the condition that Shahaji would stay in Bangalore, far away in the south. So in 1636, when Shivaji was 6, his dad left to become the governor of Bangalore. He married another woman and didn't see Shivaji and his mom for many years.

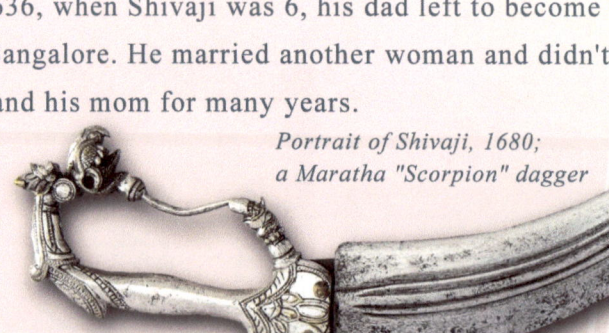

Portrait of Shivaji, 1680; a Maratha "Scorpion" dagger

10 years later, in 1646, a messenger arrived at the royal palace in Bijapur and informed the Sultan that some self-proclaimed *raja* (king), Shivaji, son of Shahaji, had occupied the fort of Torna that belonged to the Sultanate of Bijapur, robbed its treasury of 200,000 gold coins, and booted out its governor. To his shock, the Sultan found out that Shivaji was only 16 years old, and that he had been calling himself "king" since age 15! That was just the beginning. With a force of 1000 supporters, Shivaji took a few more forts in the Maratha country. He stormed some of them, and bribed others to surrender. At the Purandar Fort two younger brothers of the governor invited Shivaji to settle the inheritance dispute between them and their older brother. They just wanted to overthrow their brother, the governor, with Shivaji's help. When Shivaji arrived at the fort, the younger brothers seized their older brother and brought him to Shivaji. They were sure he would jail the governor and let them manage the fort. Instead, Shivaji threw all three of them into jail, and replaced the fort garrison with his own men.

Shivaji's "troops" – that initially were rumored to be a gang of highway robbers – started gaining battle experience and self-organized into a skilled assault force. More areas and towns were taken and now Shivaji found himself ruling over a decently-sized province. He believed that Maratha should be an independent state. As the news traveled slowly in that era, by the time messengers with the reports about Shivaji's raids came to Bijapur, Shivaji's agents were already there, bribing

the Sultan's advisors. So the reports of Shivaji's conquests never reached the Sultan's ears until one day, when devastating news came from the princedom of Kalyan. Kalyan had been recently conquered by the Bijapur Sultanate, and its new governor gathered all the contents of its treasury, as well as gold from its temples and sent all of it to the Bijapur court. The Bijapur government was eagerly awaiting the caravan from Kalyan. But no caravan ever arrived. It had been seized and robbed by Shivaji!
That was it. The Sultan of Bijapur ordered Shivaji's dad to be locked up in a dungeon cell. The door of the cell was immediately filled with bricks and only a tiny window remained through which the guards passed food to Shahaji.

"Shivaji at the the siege of Panhala fort" by M.V. Dhurandhar

"If your son doesn't stop robbing our forts, this window will be bricked too," Shahaji was told. He sent a desperate letter to his wild teenage son, and Shivaji stopped attacking Bijapur. A year later Shahaji was released. The Bijapur Sultanate couldn't afford to lose one of its best military commanders. Right away Shivaji resumed his raids on the Bijapur lands. The Bijapur government assembled an army to destroy Shivaji – under the command of their veteran general Afzal Khan. Afzal Khan laughed and laughed when he learned that he was being dispatched to fight a robber kid from Maratha. "The rascal will be brought to the Sultan in chains and tossed under the footstool of the throne," he promised.

Afzal Khan started by plundering the temple of the Hindu goddess Bhavani – a site considered holy in Shivaji's family. He continued by sweeping the Maratha countryside, hunting for Shivaji's supporters, and, finally, cornered Shivaji himself into Pratapgad Fort sitting on the top of a mountain. However, after 2 months of siege the fort was still standing and Afzal Khan still waited at the bottom of the mountain. His cavalry was useless on the rocky cliffs. In the fort, Shivaji's men ran out of food and water, and started talking about surrender. At that point Shivaji knew his situation was desperate. With his usual resourcefulness, he came up with a cunning scheme to trick Afzal Khan. He reached out to the Bijapur general asking for negotiations. Afzal Khan sent one of his trusted men, a Brahmin, to visit Shivaji. During the meeting, Shivaji assured the Brahmin that he was about to surrender, and he just wanted to ask Afzal Khan to use his influence on the Sultan to get Shivaji pardoned. Afzal Khan was vain and arrogant enough to believe that the "mountain rat" had given up, and consented to meet with Shivaji. It was agreed that Afzal Khan and Shivaji would arrive at a secret location each accompanied by only one officer and armed only with a sword. Shivaji, however, had a plan of his own.

Pratapgad Fort

He wore armor underneath his clothes and had a crooked dagger called "the scorpion" hidden in his right sleeve. On the fingers of his left hand he wore a "tiger claw," rings with a set of curved hooks made of steel – a weapon that could be easily concealed in a closed hand. His officer had two swords hidden in his sash. When Afzal Khan arrived at the meeting location, Shivaji attacked him. Afzal Khan fought back, but Shivaji wrestled him to the ground and killed him. His officer blew a horn – a signal to the Maratha troops to leave the fort and assault the Bijapur army. Taken by surprise, the Bijapur soldiers fled in panic and disorder. 3000 of them were killed and dozens taken prisoner, including two sons of Afzal Khan and his top officers. The next morning Shivaji held a great celebration for his men, and rewarded them with the Bijapur gold. He was equally generous to the Bijapur prisoners. All the captured enemy officers and Afzal Khan's sons were given food, gold, gifts and sent to their homes.

More Bijapur troops were dispatched to fight Shivaji, but Shivaji kept winning battles. Finally the tales of his daring raids and victories reached the Mughal throne. The Mughals joined forces with the Bijapur army and in 1660 Shivaji suffered a defeat in the fort of Panhala. His enemies bombarded the fort with grenades they had purchased from the British East India Company in Rajapur. More than that, the British sent their own artillerymen to operate the cannons that shelled Shivaji's forces, and they flew the British flag. Shivaji was forced to surrender the fort. In revenge he raided a trading post run by the British East India Company in Surat and captured a few British officials. Shivaji kept them imprisoned until 1663 when the East India Company got in touch with him and explained that the grenades had been sold to his enemies without the company's permission.

Meanwhile, in the Mughal Empire they crowned a new emperor – Aurangzeb. Aurangzeb had a reputation of being a merciless and vindictive individual, said to mistrust any man not imprisoned or beheaded.

Indian Bagh Nakh – Tiger Claw; Shivaji kills Afzal Khan, 19th-century painting

Aurangzeb had overthrown and jailed his old father and killed three of his brothers who dared to claim the throne. Aurangzeb had no tolerance for the Hindus in his empire. He made them pay outrageously heavy taxes. Many Hindu temples were plundered and burned, and when crowds gathered to protest and defend their places of worship, battle elephants were sent against them, to trample them to death. Under Aurangzeb's rule, the Mughal Empire was expanding faster than ever. Mughal armies pushed its borders into the few Indian states still remaining independent. To Aurangzeb, Shivaji was just another Hindu rebel from a faraway province. He had to be erased together with his dreams of Maratha's independence. So the emperor sent a force of 150 thousand, led by his uncle, Shaista Khan, to wipe out Shivaji and his entire "mountain rats" army.

The campaign started well. Shivaji's kingdom of Pune fell with little resistance and Shaista Khan moved into Shivaji's own palace, built by his father! That was very convenient, because Shaista Khan didn't like to sacrifice comfort and luxury on military expeditions and brought with him a bunch of his wives, as well as dozens of servants, cooks, and even musicians. In 1663, for the anniversary of Emperor Aurangzeb's coronation, Shaista Khan gave a great feast to his top officers. In the middle of the feast the guests heard loud music outside and were amused to see a large wedding procession passing by the palace. At the same moment Shaista Khan's musicians received a request to play music even louder – as loud as they could – to "honor the emperor." They didn't pay attention to the fact that the request was delivered by a stranger who immediately vanished. The horns blared and the kettle drums thundered, and nobody heard the shrieks of terror from the women's quarters. That's where Shivaji, accompanied by 400 armed men disguised as a wedding procession, broke into the palace.

Seconds later, with his sword drawn, Shivaji stood in front of Shaista Khan! Shaista Khan's servants swept oil lamps to the floor and in total darkness the Mughal general dashed to the window and jumped out.

"Shaista Khan surprised" by M.V. Dhurandhar

But the window was on the second floor, and for a few moments Shaista Khan was clinging to the window sill, hanging off it. That's when Shivaji reached the window and slashed Shaista Khan's hand holding to the window sill with his sword, chopping off three of the general's fingers! Shivaji and his men set the Mughal camp on fire and vanished before Shaista Khan's officers reached it. When Emperor Aurangzeb learned about this embarrassment, he punished his uncle by transferring him to a lower government position in Bengal.

To refill his empty treasury, Shivaji plundered the coastal Portuguese colony of Basrur and kept on fighting the Mughals. Aurangzeb tried to entrap Shivaji. He ordered his eldest son, Prince Shah Alam, to lead his army to the Deccan and then to pretend that he turned against his father. Shah Alam announced that he was gathering troops for a revolt against the emperor and reached out to the Marathas inviting them to fight on his side. Indeed, many joined him, but Shivaji figured out it was a trap and sat it out in his stronghold in the mountains. The moment the prince received a "No" from Shivaji, his "rebellion" was suddenly over and his father "pardoned" him. But the Marathas who had joined the fake rebellion were all beheaded by Prince Shah Alam.

In 1665 yet another Mughal army headed south to hunt Shivaji. This time, Aurangzeb had a new strategy: What he couldn't achieve by the sword, he would achieve with the gold. While besieging Shivaji's forts, the Mughal general Jai Singh secretly reached out to Shivaji's commanders offering them a pardon from the emperor, high ranks in the Mughal army and rich rewards for switching sides. Many agreed and accepted his offer. Shivaji's army was melting and shrinking and he was cornered in yet another tiny fortress on a mountain cliff – Purandar. Jai Singh offered to negotiate. He promised Shivaji pardon and protection by the emperor if Shivaji accepted the Mughal rule. He gave Shivaji his word of honor that Shivaji and his family wouldn't be harmed.

"On the way to Purandar," Shivaji talks to his troops, by M.V. Dhurandhar

Days passed in drafting a deal, and finally Shivaji signed the Treaty of Purandar, surrendering to the Mughals 23 of his forts and the Mughal lands he had seized. He was to become a *vassal* (a subordinate) of the Mughal Empire. In return he received the right to collect and keep taxes in a few districts of the Maratha country. Emperor Aurangzeb was thrilled, and so – actually – was Shivaji. The areas he surrendered were the poorest, while the districts he was allowed to tax were the wealthiest. Shivaji would not be Shivaji if he gave in to the Mughals! But the road to Maratha independence and his own Maratha Empire was long. Shivaji's greatest victories still lay ahead of him. At the signing of the treaty, Shivaji was 35 years old. He had 4 wives, 8 children, and a fighting spirit that burned in his heart like fire – brighter and hotter with every passing year.

Ever since Shivaji started fighting the Mughals, he had had a dream. He wanted to visit the Mughal capitals, Agra and Delhi, and see the splendor of the imperial court. He was also interested in leading his army on a Mughal military campaign in Afghanistan to replenish his treasury with plunder. One day Aurangzeb received a messenger from Shivaji with a letter in which Shivaji asked permission for him and his 9-year-old son Sambhaji to visit Agra. "Bid him come," responded the emperor.

"Shivaji at Aurangzeb's court" by M.V. Dhurandhar

The Peacock Throne (from a Mughal painting)

Shivaji had high expectations for this trip, but Aurangzeb, disdainful and vengeful, saw this as an opportunity to demonstrate to Shivaji what a worthless provincial nobody Shivaji was, and also, that as Aurangzeb's subject, he was now no better than a servant. Aurangzeb really wanted to rub it in. When Shivaji drew near the capital he expected to be met by some high officials of the royal court, as custom required, but only a couple of inferior-rank officers showed up. Shivaji had to wait in Agra for Aurangzeb to give him an audience for three months! But the audience itself was even more humiliating.

Aurangzeb sat on a golden platform, on his famous Peacock Throne, sparkling with gems. His robes and turban were dripping with diamonds and rubies. Shivaji had never seen such magnificence before. Dozens of court officials stood in lines facing the emperor. Shivaji found himself at the end of one such line, and it didn't even look like the emperor knew he was there or was planning to speak with him. Even worse, ahead of him Shivaji recognized some low-ranking Mughal military commanders whom he had defeated in battles! Right away he knew that this was a show designed to humiliate him. Shivaji couldn't hold back his indignation. He stepped out of the line and addressed the emperor with a bitter speech, pointing out the mean-spirited manner in which he was treated. He finished by accusing the emperor's courtiers and generals of being slavish flatterers and stormed out of the reception hall. Shivaji was immediately grabbed and placed under house arrest.

The Peacock Throne

During Nowruz, the Iranian New Year celebration, Mughal officials brought gifts of gems to the members of the imperial family. In exchange they received promotions in the government and high ranks in the Mughal army. By the time Akbar's grandson, Shah Jahan, became the emperor, his treasury had so many jewels that he decided to use them to decorate his throne. His famous Peacock Throne was designed and built in 1635. It was of solid gold, with lots of sapphires, rubies, emeralds, and pearls sparkling all over it. On top of its canopy there were figures of dancing peacocks. Among the gems that adorned the peacocks' heads was the famous Koh-i-Noor, one of the biggest diamonds in the world.

Aurangzeb was satisfied that Shivaji was now in his hands and casually considered murdering him. But there was an obstacle. Shivaji was guarded by one of the sons of Jai Singh who had given Shivaji his word of honor that he would be safe as the Mughal vassal. The emperor valued Jai Singh and didn't want to upset him. A couple months passed, and suddenly Aurangzeb received a request from Jai Singh's son to dismiss him from guarding Shivaji. He had some family business to attend elsewhere. Aurangzeb granted him permission to leave. The next day he was told that Shivaji was sick and was likely to die soon. Shivaji humbly asked the emperor for permission to send gifts to Hindu temples as offerings to gods in hope of healing. The emperor rolled his eyes and sent word to Shivaji that gifts to temples were allowed. Every day huge baskets were filled with fruit and flowers in the courtyard of the guest house where Shivaji and his son were staying. After a couple weeks the soldiers guarding the house got used to seeing the baskets leaving the courtyard every morning. Nobody thought much of it until one day Shivaji disappeared. He packaged himself and his son into the baskets under heaps of flowers. The baskets were carried by his servants past the guards, down the crowded street to the outskirts of the city. Over there the horses waited for them, and days later Shivaji was in the Deccan. Dressed as a Hindu pilgrim, he made way to the Maratha country, to his own kingdom of Pune. There he started to assemble his forces to fight the Mughals once again.

A year later Aurangzeb realized that alienating Shivaji had been a blunder. Having Shivaji on his side was better than fighting the growing Maratha forces. He officially gave Shivaji the title of raja and more lands to collect taxes for his income. But the peace lasted only for 2-3 years, while Shivaji was rebuilding his army. Meanwhile, yet another rebellion flared up in Mughal provinces in Afghanistan. To battle the Afghan rebels, Aurangzeb pulled his troops from the Deccan. Many Hindu soldiers, who served the Mughals, unwilling to leave the Deccan, joined Shivaji's army. In 1670 Shivaji led his men to invade the lands he had surrendered under the Treaty of Purandar. Only 4 months later he recaptured most of these territories and plundered English trading posts in Surat and Bombay for refusing to sell weapons to him.

Even more victories followed, and in 1674 Shivaji was crowned king of his new, independent Maratha Kingdom, with the title "the Protector of the Hindu Faith." The ceremony, held at Shivaji's capital, Raigad Fort, was solemn and magnificent. At the end, following an ancient custom, Shivaji was weighed, and his weight in gold was distributed among the Brahmins.

Shivaji's signature from a letter written in 1674

Shivaji's son and the heir to the Maratha crown, Sambhaji, was a rebel like his dad. When he grew up, he refused to play by Shivaji's rules and at some point Shivaji was so angry with him, he grabbed Sambhaji and his wife and locked them up at Panhala Fort. But Sambhaji took after his dad in more ways than one. He and his wife escaped from the fort and defected to Aurangzeb. However, after a year in the Mughal service, Sambhaji returned to Maratha. Soon he was arrested and imprisoned by Shivaji once again. A year later Shivaji died. He was only 50, and many suspected that he had been poisoned by his second wife Soyarabai who wanted to crown her 10-year-old son King of Maratha – instead of Sambhaji. Indeed, after Shivaji's death, she talked influential men at the court to proclaim her son king, and he was crowned. But Sambhaji escaped from his guards at Panhala Fort, killed the fort commander, gathered a band of supporters, and seized the Maratha throne.

Firearms in India

Firearms were invented in China, in the 10th century. The first guns were bamboo or metal tubes filled with gunpowder and "bullets," such as scraps of metal, or bits of broken porcelain. In the 13th century Arab and Mamluk armies started using firearms, and a century later the firearm technology reached Europe.

The first recorded use of firearms in India occurred in 1368 when the Bahmani Sultanate used cannons against the Vijayanagara Empire. When the Portuguese started to colonize India in the early 16th century, they brought with them European cannons and muskets. Around the same time Babur brought Turkish firearms technology to India. However, both colonists and invaders reported that the Indians already had their own firearms, such as simple handguns manufactured by blacksmiths. Despite the availability of the firearms, Indian troops actively used bows all the way into the 18th century. The bows disappeared only after the guns were improved enough to significantly shorten their loading time.

*"Promise of Tanaji" by M.V. Dhurandhar
Shivaji's mom gives her blessing to Tanaji Malusare, Shivaji's friend and a general in his army. Shivaji is sad about the Treaty of Purandar that gave the Mughal Empire some of the best Maratha forts. To cheer him up, Tanaji (kneeling) promises one day he would return the Maratha lands.*

Tipu Sultan
1751 – 1799

Tipu Sultan was a ruler of the Sultanate of Mysore in southeastern India. He is best known for fighting 3 wars against the British East India Company. There are clashing opinions on Tipu Sultan's role in Indian history. Some historians view him as a national hero, a true patriot and an independence fighter. Of many Indian rulers who faced the British, Tipu was virtually the only one who refused any deals and bribes and died fighting the colonizers. Others point out that to fight the British, Tipu joined forces with the French who were also trying to colonize India. So he sided with one group of invaders against another group of invaders. What if the British had lost, and India had become a French colony? Would Tipu Sultan still have been considered a hero?

After the death of Emperor Aurangzeb in 1707 the Mughal Empire broke into pieces, and the European colonizers – the British East India Company and the French East India Company – intensified their push into India. First came the three Carnatic Wars fought by the British against the remnants of the Mughal Empire and against the French East India Company on the east coast of India, in its Carnatic region. More wars followed, and soon the British controlled most ports on both the east and west coasts of the Indian Subcontinent. As they started expanding their reach inland, they clashed with Hyder Ali, the ruler of the Kingdom of Mysore and Tipu Sultan's father.

Hyder Ali was a Muslim military commander in the service of the Hindu King of Mysore. After years of power struggle around the throne, Hyder Ali overthrew and imprisoned the king of Mysore and proclaimed himself the Sultan. Hyder Ali was illiterate, but he hired the best teachers for his kids. Tipu grew up speaking Persian, Arabic, and Kannada in addition to his native Urdu, and studying the Quran, law, and military arts. His classes in military training were taught by French officers who served in the French colonial troops.

At age 15, in 1766, Tipu Sultan fought against the British in the First Anglo-Mysore War with his own force of 3000 men. He showed such bravery and tactical skill that his dad appointed him the commander of one of his best cavalry units and made him the governor of 2 districts of his kingdom.

Hyder Ali pushed back the British, but peace never came. The Maratha Empire invaded Mysore from the North. Tipu, still a teenager, was sent on missions that didn't bring much military glory, such as setting crops on fire, poisoning wells in Maratha-occupied territories, and forcing local villagers to leave their homes and stay in refugee camps. Eventually Hyder Ali's army suffered a defeat and fled under artillery fire all the way to Mysore capital, Srirangapatna.

Almost captured by the enemy, Tipu threw away his gold royal armor and dressed as a beggar to escape. Hyder Ali avoided captivity thanks to one of his generals who, posing as Hyder Ali, surrendered to the Marathas and kept them deceived for 10 days. This gave Hyder Ali a chance to escape and hide in a small mosque near Srirangapatna. At first he thought his son had perished, but when Tipu suddenly showed up at the mosque, Hyder Ali was so happy he gave two handfuls of gold to every Mysore soldier who survived, and to every cavalry man who escaped the slaughter with his horse he gave five handfuls of gold.

The Second Anglo-Mysore War was the most successful for Hyder Ali and Tipu Sultan. The British captured the port of Mahe on the East coasts of India. The port had been controlled by the French and defended by French and Mysorean troops. Tipu Sultan responded by attacking the British. The East India Company's armies usually consisted of a few hundred Brits, mostly cavalry, and a few thousand **sepoys** – Indian foot soldiers. Tipu Sultan typically sought to take the Europeans prisoner and kill as many native soldiers as he could. The British were defeated. Hundreds of their officers were locked up in Mysore's prisons for years. During the war Hyder Ali died and in 1782 Tipu Sultan was crowned the Sultan of Mysore.

One of the factors that contributed to Mysore's success was the invention of the first-ever iron-cased **Mysorean rockets** developed in a special laboratory set up by Tipu Sultan. Rockets – "fire arrows" – were invented in China, in the 14th century. Europeans adopted Chinese rocket weapons in their original form – with their containers constructed from paper. Mysoreans were the first to use metal tubes to hold the explosive

A Mysorean soldier with a rocket laucher and a flag of Mysore attached to it – a drawing by Robert Home

(black powder) which increased the range of the rockets to 1.2 miles (2km). The rocket container tube, about 8 inches (20 cm) long, was attached to a bamboo stick. The stick was used to set an angle for the rocket trajectory. Mysorean rocket men calculated that angle from the diameter of the rocket cylinder and an approximate distance to the target. Mysoreans also invented the first multiple rocket launcher – a wheeled device that shot up to 10 rockets almost simultaneously. Mysorean rockets were used to set fire to British fortifications, explode their arsenals and destroy their *vanguard* units from a safe distance (vanguard = soldiers at the head of an advancing army).

Despite the many military successes of the Mysore Kingdom under the rule of Tipu Sultan, the threat from the British was only growing. It didn't help that the Maratha Hindus and non-Muslim population of Mysore hated Tipu Sultan. Whenever he conquered a new town he forced the local population to convert to Islam and to serve in his troops. A Mysore government official, Ramachandra Rao, reported about the forced

"Mysorean rockets," a vintage illustration

conversion of Christians in Mangalore: "Thirty or forty thousand native Christians of Mangalore were sent by Tipu as prisoners to Srirangapatna, where they were kept as converts." The 27 Christian churches in Mangalore were burned down, the priests thrown in jail. The lands that belonged to the Christians were confiscated and redistributed among Tipu Sultan's commanders and officials.

Another reason Tipu Sultan had no support among the common people in the lands he controlled were the extreme measures he took to make these lands unattractive to European colonists.

Hindi and Urdu

Urdu and Hindi are languages of the Indo-European family widely spoken in India. Urdu – the national language of Pakistan – is the 10th most spoken language in the world, while Hindi – the official language of India – is the world's 4th most spoken language. Speakers of Urdu and Hindi understand each other, even though a lot of Urdu vocabulary comes from the Persian language, Farsi, spoken in Iran, while a lot of Hindi vocabulary comes from Sanskrit. The writing systems of these two languages are different: Hindi is written in the Indian Devanagari script (left-to-right), while Urdu uses Persian alphabet derived from Arabic script (right-to-left).

"General Lord Cornwallis receiving Tipu Sultan's sons as hostages" by Robert Home, 1793

Hamilton-Buchanan, an English traveler who visited Mysore in the 1810s and 1820s, writes that Tipu destroyed crops that Europeans were interested in purchasing or seizing for export to Europe. For example, writing about the Kanara region, he observes, "They say, that Tipu, in order to remove every reason for Europeans to come to this area, destroyed all the pepper vines, and all the trees which supported them." It was not surprising that Tipu Sultan had to constantly dispatch troops to various corners of his kingdom to suppress revolts. Sending one of his commanders, Badr-uz-zaman Khan, to deal with rebels in Kanara, Tipu wrote: "Ten years ago, from 10 to 15 thousand men were hung upon the trees of that district. Since then those trees have been waiting for more. You must therefore hang upon those trees all the inhabitants of that district that have led the rebellion."

The third Anglo-Mysore War was disastrous for Tipu Sultan. His enemies – the British and the Marathas joined forces and attacked on all fronts simultaneously. Tipu Sultan lost nearly half of his kingdom and had to send two of his sons as hostages to the British until he paid a war *indemnity* (cash compensation paid by the losing side). Devastated, Tipu Sultan found an unusual way to cheer himself up. He ordered his craftsmen to create an "automaton" (a mechanical toy or model) depicting a tiger mauling a British soldier. Today this automaton is at the Victoria and Albert Museum in London. When it is activated, the soldier raises his hand as if trying to defend himself, while making screaming noises, and the tiger growls.

The automaton was inspired by an actual event that happened in 1792: British officer Lieutenant Hugh Monro was killed by a tiger on a picnic in Indian woods. The tiger also symbolized the power of Mysore and stood for Tipu Sultan himself, since Tipu had a nickname – the Tiger of Mysore. According to legend, one day, while hunting, he was attacked by a tiger. He grabbed his gun, but the gun got jammed and failed. Tipu held off the tiger with his bare hands until he managed to draw a dagger. The tiger became his emblem. Tipu even kept tigers as pets in his palace.

In 1798 Napoleon landed in Egypt hoping to make it a launchpad for the invasion of India. Along with their native allies, including Tipu Sultan, Napoleonic troops were supposed to drive the British off the Indian coasts. But Napoleon's Egyptian campaign failed, and Tipu Sultan was left practically alone defending what was left of Mysore against the East India Company and the Marathas. His capital, Srirangapatna, was besieged by a British army of 60 thousand under the command of General David Baird who had been captured by Tipu Sultan in the Second Anglo-Mysore War and held in prison for 4 years. Inside the Srirangapatna fortress Tipu Sultan had only 30 thousand soldiers.

The British bribed Tipu's minister Mir Sadiq and he pointed the enemy to a spot where the walls of the city could be breached. Shooting across the River Cauvery, the British artillery blasted a hole in the inner wall of Srirangapatna and General Baird sent a secret message to Mir Sadiq saying that the British would storm the city at noon. So at noon Mir Sadiq locked Tipu Sultan in one of the defensive towers and pretended he was about to distribute pay to the Mysorean troops who were guarding the breach in the wall. The moment they withdrew into the city, where they were to receive their pay, Mir Sadiq appeared on the wall and waved a white handkerchief – a sign to the British to start the attack. Leading the charge were the so-called "forlorn hopes" ("hope-left-behind" soldiers), fighters who performed suicide missions, such as climbing up the fortress walls or leading attacks against well-defended fortifications.

Tipu Sultan's Tiger automaton

The 76 "forlorn hopes," well-fueled with whiskey, crossed the river which was only about 4 feet (1.2m) deep, climbed the low outer wall and rushed toward the breach in the inner wall of the city. Tipu Sultan broke out of the tower where he was locked and perished in a hand-to-hand combat at one of the gates. Srirangapatna fell. Mir Sadiq was killed by the surviving Mysorean soldiers when he walked out to greet the British troops after the city had been conquered. Srirangapatna residents, enraged by his betrayal, dug his body out of the grave and dragged it around the city for days. Even today Indian tourists visiting Srirangapatna throw stones at the spot on the city street where Mir Sadiq was killed, and hurl shoes at his tomb.

In Srirangapatna the British found hundreds of Mysorean rockets of a few different designs and sent them to the Royal Arsenal in London to be *reverse-engineered*. As a result, Mysorean rockets were adopted by the British army, and in 1804 the British started industrial manufacturing of military rockets. These weapons were used in the wars against Napoleon and against the United States during the War of 1812.

Reverse Engineering

Reverse engineering is disassembling a product to see how it works and copying its design to produce more products like this. It's "reverse," because engineers work backward, developing the design based on a finished product.

"The storming of Srirangapatna" by Richard Caton Woodville

Ranjit Singh
1780 – 1839

Ranjit Singh, nicknamed the Lion of Lahore, was the founder and first **Maharaja** (ruler) of the Sikh Empire in Punjab, northwest India. He succeeded in unifying numerous Sikh princedoms and confederacies and brought an era of economic modernization, prosperity, and cultural "renaissance" (rebirth).

Ranjit Singh was born to a princely Sikh family. His name, Ranjit, means "a winner in battle." Singh means "a lion." In early childhood he lost his vision in one eye due to smallpox. That's why in some of his portraits he looks like he is winking. Ranjit's education focused on military arts. He studied the alphabet of the Punjabi language, but never really learned to read or write. When Ranjit Singh was 9, his parents arranged a "marriage" for him. His bride was a girl whose father had perished in a battle against Ranjit's dad, in a war between two Sikh "misls" – clans. The warring clans decided to seal their peace agreement with a marriage hoping that family ties would prevent another war. Arranged "marriages" between kids were common. They held the marriage ceremony, but after the wedding the "bride" went home with her parents. Usually many years later, when kids grew up, the families celebrated the "muklawa" – the bride and groom moving in together.

At 10 Ranjit started accompanying his dad on military expeditions. During the siege of Manchar fort, riding on an elephant with one of his father's warriors, Ranjit was spotted by a Manchar fighter who was trying to make his way into the fort on horseback. The Manchar soldier sneaked close to the elephant, jumped on its back and drew out his sword. Fortunately, Ranjit's companion fought him off, saving Ranjit's life.

Ranjit became the chief of his Sikh clan at 12, when his father died. At 16 he invited his wife, Mehtab Kaur, to move in with him, but their marriage didn't last. She never forgave Ranjit's family for her father's death, and eventually returned to live with her mother, Sada Kaur, who had become the leader of her clan after her husband's death. It was common for Sikh rulers to have many wives, and Ranjit Singh is said to have married 20 times! Most of these marriages were political deals whose purpose was to strengthen military alliances or assure the loyalty of powerful Sikh families.

Ranjit Singh's wives came from every religious background. Some of them were Hindu. They kept their faith and were not required to convert to Sikhism. Religious tolerance was vital to Ranjit Singh's success. After the death of Aurangzeb (1707) the Mughal Empire started crumbling. Afghan warlords were raiding Punjab more and more often. To drive them back, it was important for the Sikhs to gain the support of both Hindus and Muslims in Punjab. The Sikhs were no longer a purely religious community. Suffering from persecution at the hands of Mughal governors, they had started forming military units and training for combat. In 1675, the Ninth Guru of Sikhism, Guru Tegh Bahadur, was seized by Aurangzeb's Muslim officials when he agreed to protect the Hindus from religious persecution by the Mughals. The Muslim officials demanded that Guru either perform a miracle to prove that he was a 'holy man,' or convert to Islam. When he refused, he was publicly beheaded. In 1699, his son, Guru Gobind Singh, the Tenth and last Sikh Guru, founded the **Khalsa** – the Sikh warrior tradition that made it an official duty of the Sikhs to protect non-Muslims from religious oppression. Gobind Singh fought 14 wars against the Mughal Empire. His fighting spirit was alive among the Sikhs when Ranjit Singh was growing up, but there was no unity among the Sikh clans.

The Khanda

The Khanda is the emblem of Sikhism. It features
- *a double-edged sword (a khanda) in the center representing the warrior code of the Khalsa*
- *two single-edged daggers (kirpans) – the unity of the spiritual and worldly realms under God's authority*
- *a circular throwing blade (a chakram) – the symbol of the eternal nature of God*

The 5 Ks

Guru Gobind Singh commanded Sikh warriors to wear or carry with them at all times these 5 items:

- *Kesh: uncut hair. Sikhs don't cut their hair. The long hair is tied in a knot and held with a wooden comb called a "kangha." The knot is usually covered with a turban. Kesh is a symbol of one's devotion to God.*
- *Kangha: a wooden comb*
- *Kara: an iron or steel bracelet – a symbol of loyalty to God*
- *Kirpan: a sword or dagger – symbol of God's power*
- *Kachera: cotton shorts worn by Sikh warriors. Unlike traditional Indian clothing, kachera didn't constrain movement, and many Sikh warriors wore only kachera in battle, although in everyday life it is worn under one's clothes.*

Below: A Sikh athlete at the 1936 Olympic Games teaches his friends how to tie a Sikh turban

Ranjit Singh became famous among Sikh misls at 17, when his strategy and courage helped the Sikhs win the Battle of Amritsar against the Afghans. That same year, 1797, another Afghan invasion followed. This time Ranjit Singh let the invading army enter Lahore, then had his troops surround the city and burn all the crops in the fields around it. Starved, the Afghans left. The Sikh clan that ruled Lahore was unpopular with its residents, especially with the Sufi Muslims and the Hindus. Ranjit's mother-in-law, Sada Kaur, suggested bringing together the troops of their clans to take over Lahore, because "whoever controls Lahore, rules Punjab." Ranjit Singh agreed, and in 1799 their joint forces approached Lahore. The residents of Lahore opened the gates for them, and the Lahore ruling family fled. Ranjit Singh took control of the city. Two years later 21-year-old Ranjit Singh proclaimed himself Maharaja of Punjab. But the first coin of his new kingdom didn't bear his name. It was stamped with the name of Guru Nanak, the founder of the Sikh faith.

In 1802 a scandal erupted at Ranjit Singh's court. He fell in love with a dancer who performed at court celebrations and started dating her. Her name was Moran. Moran was beautiful, educated, and a good conversationalist, but she came from a poor family, she was dating a married man, and she was a Muslim! One of Ranjit Singh's advisors asked him to send Moran away from the court, but Ranjit Singh became furious, threw him in jail, confiscated all his lands, and married Moran. Ranjit's first wife cried and protested. The second moved out to live with her parents. The scandal reached Amritsar and outraged the Sikh community of the Golden Temple, the main Sikh holy site and house of worship.

"A dancing girl" by Edwin Lord Weeks

In 1708 Guru Gobind Singh declared that there would be no more gurus in Sikhism. The religious authority was transferred to the entire Sikh community whose representatives met at Akal Takht, the religious council building near the Golden Temple. Ranjit Singh was summoned to Akal Takht where the chief priest convicted him of violating the social rules of Sikhism. Ranjit Singh begged the community to forgive him, but was declared guilty and sentenced to one hundred lash strikes on his bare back in front of the whole town. Ranjit Singh took off his shirt and they tied him to a tamarind tree near Akal Takht. Among the people who had gathered to watch the punishment, many burst into tears. Seeing this, the chief priest addressed the crowd: "Sikh warriors! The maharaja has accepted the punishment that you decided to inflict upon him. But he is after all our king. We should honor his position. I suggest that he should be given only one strike on his back as a token of his submission to the majesty of our social law." The crowd cheered, Ranjit Singh received his one strike, was untied from the tree, and bowed to the people of Amritsar. Everyone was treated to sweet pudding and went home.

Indian author and traveler, Husain Shahi, wrote in 1796, "In the country of the Punjab, from the Indus to the banks of the Yamuna, there are thousands of Sikh chiefs. None obeys the other. If a person owns two or three horses, he boasts of being a sardar, and is ready to fight against thousands."

Sardar

The word 'sardar' came from Farsi, the Persian language spoken in Iran, where it means "a commander." In Punjab 'Sardar' became the title of Sikh clan leaders, and later came to be used as a respectful form of address.

"Ranjit Singh listening to the reading from the Granth Sahib, the holy book of the Sikhs" by August Schoefft, 1850

Many of these Sikh clans, however, were powerful, had armies counting dozens of thousands of troops, and didn't hesitate attacking each other. Their sardars refused to recognize Ranjit Singh as their ruler. To turn them into allies and, later, his subjects, Ranjit Singh used two methods. One was to marry a clan chief's daughter. That's why Ranjit Singh had so many wives! Being a maharaja's father-in-law was an honor. But the custom required that the parents of the bride offer her future husband a dowry. To marry Sikh princesses, Ranjit Singh demanded large chunks of their clan territory to be transferred to him as dowry. This grew the lands he controlled and weakened the clans of his new relatives. The other method was a "vow of brotherhood." The maharaja and a clan leader exchanged turbans and swore on the Sikh holy book, the Granth, to treat each other as brothers. Becoming the maharaja's brother came with an obligation. Sardars promised to fight in Ranjit Singh's wars and expand his empire.

With less powerful chiefs, Ranjit Singh took a less diplomatic approach. Traveling around Punjab, whenever he stopped, he demanded that the local sardars come and stay with him at his camp. If any of them failed to arrive right away, they were declared traitors. Their land and treasures were seized and added to the maharaja's property. Occasionally, Ranjit Singh used deception to get rid of Sikh clan leaders. In 1802 he invited Jodh Singh, the ruler of Wazirabad, to visit him in Lahore. Jodh Singh had fought in the maharaja's wars against the Afghans, but he didn't trust Ranjit Singh one bit and came accompanied by a few hundred of his best fighters. It is reported that when Ranjit Singh offered him to exchange turbans in a "vow of brotherhood," Jodh Singh replied, "May I be excused from this honor? I'll consider myself lucky if I can keep my own turban and my head." Ranjit Singh, however, treated his guest so warmly, with such friendliness, that Jodh Singh sent back his troops leaving only 25 soldiers to guard him. Immediately, Ranjit Singh ordered his men to capture Jodh Singh. But when they broke the door in the house where Jodh Singh stayed, he stood up with his back to the wall, drew his sword and shouted, "Come on, you will never take me alive. I don't know how to turn my back on an enemy!" Ranjit Singh was so impressed with his bravery, he pretended that the attack was a mistake and sent Jodh Singh home with rich presents.

Ranjit Singh won a number of military campaigns against the Afghans, expanded his empire toward Afghanistan, and conquered Kashmir. He also made a deal with the British East India Company. Both promised not to cross the Sutlej River, the border between the Sikh lands and the British colonial territories. French botanist Victor Jacquemont visited Lahore in 1831 and reported the following conversation with Ranjit Singh.

"What conquests should I undertake?" wondered the maharaja. "Any country not already occupied by the English," suggested the Frenchman. "Maybe Tibet? You've traveled there. What do you think?" continued Ranjit Singh. "That will be easy. It's a very poor country," answered Jacquemont. Then Ranjit Singh exclaimed, "But what's the use of conquering such a country? I want lands that are rich and prosperous!"

Ranjit Singh was an efficient and just ruler. He gave Muslims and Hindus some of the top positions in his government and met with common people listening to their suggestions and grievances (complaints). The problem was, he didn't have time to listen to everyone, and when he suggested that people send their complaints to his government in writing, it turned out that most of them were illiterate. And so, Ranjit Singh, who couldn't read or write himself, made it his goal to increase literacy in Punjab. He ordered scholars to create a textbook teaching Farsi (Persian) and basic math. 5000 copies of this book were distributed to schools across Punjab, and after some years 87% of Lahore, and 78% of Punjab could read in Farsi and count.

Ranjit Singh believed in fate, witchcraft, lucky and unlikely numbers, and omens. Before proceeding with his government projects or military campaigns, he always consulted his court astrologers. Sometimes he had his advisors write potential outcomes – success or failure – on two sheets of paper, put them on the Granth, the Sikh holy book, and had a little kid pick one of the sheets without looking at it. If he picked the "failure" sheet, Ranjit Singh postponed or canceled the project. Once he fell ill, and his astrologers told him that he was currently being harmed by the planet Saturn. To block the influence of Saturn, they suggested that Ranjit Singh find a Brahmin who, representing Saturn, would ride a black horse and leave Punjab forever. They found a Brahmin, covered his body and face with soot, dressed him in black clothes, and put him on a black horse. The maharaja gave him gold earrings and a large gift of money. The Brahmin was escorted out of the Sikh lands by two regiments of soldiers. Wherever he rode, people closed the doors of their houses to prevent the "Saturn" from harming them.

Ranjit Singh's throne

One of the entertainments at Ranjit Singh's court was his famous Beard Show. The Sikh nobles competed to see who had the longest beard, and the maharaja gave them prizes.

Koh-i-Noor

The Koh-i-Noor is one of the largest cut diamonds in the world (105.6 carats, or 21.12 grams). It is first mentioned in historical sources as one of the gems that decorated the famous Peacock Throne of the Mughal Empire. In 1739 Nader Shah, the shah of Iran, defeated the Mughal army and entered Delhi. His biographers say that when he saw the famous diamond on the Peacock Throne, he exclaimed in Persian, "Koh-i-Noor!" which means "The mountain of light!" – giving the diamond its name. Nader Shah was assassinated. Koh-i-Noor changed hands a few times, and in 1813 it was given to Ranjit Singh by an Afghan ruler who had been overthrown and had come to Lahore as a refugee. Ranjit Singh wore the Koh-i-Noor on his turban and also on an armlet – an armband decorated with gems. Ranjit Singh was always afraid that the Koh-i-Noor could be stolen, so when it was to be transported, it was carried on a camel in a caravan of 39 camels and nobody except Ranjit Singh's treasurer knew which camel carried the diamond. After Punjab was annexed by the East India Company, the Koh-i-Noor diamond was given to Queen Victoria.

Koh-i-Noor on Ranjit Singh's armlet

William Osborne, a British military officer and diplomat, described a reception of the British mission – visiting diplomats – at the court of Ranjit Singh in his book *Court and Camp of Ranjit Singh*: "The floor was covered with rich silk carpets. A gorgeous fabric canopy, embroidered with gold and precious stones, supported on golden pillars was placed in a garden. Every pathway was lined with troops. The Maharaja's courtiers stood behind him. In front there were leading nobles, Sikhs, Hindus, and Muslims, chiefs from Kabul and Kandahar, all blazing with gold and jewels, and dressed and armed in a delightful variety of color and fashion. The maharaja sat cross-legged in a golden chair. He wore simple white clothes, without ornaments. He had a single string of enormous pearls around his waist, and the Koh-i-Noor on his arm. The mountain of light and his fiery eye competed with each other in brilliance. His chiefs all squatted on the floor around his chair. One hour was spent in pleasant conversation. Then the maharaja rose. He sprinkled sandalwood scent on the clothes of the mission. He embraced them and allowed them to leave with ceremonies."

Osborne also reported a few conversations he had with Ranjit Singh. Once Ranjit Singh asked Osborne, "How many troops have you got in this country altogether?"
"About 200,000," Osborne replied. "20 or at the most, 30 thousand British troops can march from one end of India to the other, and no power in the country can stop them."
"And how many Frenchmen can an Englishman beat?" inquired the maharaja.
"At school, in England, the boys are always taught to consider themselves equal to three Frenchmen," responded Osborne.

"What about the Russians?...If the Russians cross the Indus River, what force can you send against them?"
"30,000 British troops and 70,000 of your Sikhs."
"Do Russians have a lot of money?"
"No, very little."
"So it'll be all fighting and nothing to plunder? Maybe they better not come."

By the end of Ranjit Singh's reign his empire was surrounded by British colonial territories and troops on three sides out of four. British diplomats and generals visited him regularly, reminding him of vultures circling around, awaiting his death. He certainly knew that sooner or later the British would move to add Punjab to their colonial possessions. This bothered the maharaja, and he drowned his anxiety in heavy drinking and opium addiction. His sons spent their days hunting, partying, and fighting with one another. They showed neither talent, nor desire to rule. In 1836, German traveler Charles Hugel wrote while visiting Lahore, "After Ranjit Singh's death disorder and anarchy will prevail, until the whole empire will become a portion of the vast dominions of British India." Ranjit Singh died of a stroke in 1839. Ten years later Punjab became a British colony.

Vintage photographs of Sikh warriors with chakrams – throwing weapons with sharpened outer edges – around their necks and other types of combat blades carried on their turbans; 19th-century chakrams.

RANI OF JHANSI
1828 – 1858

Rani of Jhansi, or Rani Laxmibai was an Indian independence fighter, a heroine of the Indian Rebellion of 1857. She is the main character of many novels, comic books, and movies. Her courage is celebrated in poetry and folk songs. In 1943, the Indian Army paid tribute to her by creating an all-women regiment in her name.

Rani of Jhansi's birth name was Manikarnika. "Rani" is the royal title – "queen" – that she received when she married the Maharaja of Jhansi. She was born in the town of Varanasi, in the Maratha Confederacy. Her father was a military commander and a government official. Her mom died when Rani was 5, and she was raised by her dad. Her best childhood friends were two boys who later became the leaders of the Indian Rebellion of 1857 – Nana Saheb and Tatya Tope. Together with them Rani studied shooting, sword fighting, archery, and horseback riding – skills that were never taught to women. Because Rani took classes with boys, she also learned reading and writing – hardly ever taught to girls in that era. Rani's biographers say that with girls she played "housekeeping" games, in which she was always a queen ordering her servants around. When boys practiced riding an elephant and refused to take her along, she cried and shouted to them, "I'll show you! For your one elephant, I will have ten. Remember my words!" Astrologers predicted a royal husband for Rani, and her dad said "no" to all marriage proposals until the Maharaja of Jhansi asked for her hand in marriage. Bride and groom walked 7 times around the sacred fire, then a priest tied together the ends of their robes. At that moment, Rani suddenly said, "Make that knot real tight!" Some guests were shocked at Rani's boldness, but the deal was done: She was now a queen. The astrologer who had predicted a royal marriage for Rani received a generous reward from her dad. After the wedding, according to custom, Rani took a new name – Lakshmibai in honor of Lakshmi, the Hindu goddess of wealth and victory.

Indian movie star Mehtab as Rani of Jhansi from a poster for the 1953 film "Jhansi Ki Rani"; Below: 19th-century solid silver bowl, India

Jhansi is a city that grew around a fort built in 1613. Together with the villages surrounding it, Jhansi was an independent princedom. Rani's husband, Maharaja Gangadhar Rao was a patron of arts and loved theater. He enjoyed acting in shows staged at his court, playing both male and female roles. Acting was considered inappropriate for women. There were no actresses. He was absorbed in theater life and costume design, and tried to ignore the distressing aspects of being a maharaja, such as dealing with the British who were circling Jhansi like a pack of hungry wolves. In 1851 Rani of Jhansi gave birth to a baby boy, but her son died in infancy, and then, a couple years later, her husband fell seriously ill with dysentery. Soon he was on his deathbed, and there was no heir to the Jhansi throne.

This was potentially catastrophic because the British couldn't wait to add Jhansi to their colonial empire. To seize more Indian states without a major war, they came up with the so-called "Doctrine of Lapse." According to this rule, if any Indian prince died without an heir, his state would "lapse" (fall) under British control. A day before the Maharaja of Jhansi died, he adopted one of his distant cousins as his son – to prevent the British from applying the "Doctrine of Lapse" to Jhansi. In the presence of an official from the British East India Company, the maharaja signed his will, leaving the throne to his cousin, Damodar Rao, who was 5 years old. The British governor-general, however, had already decided to seize Jhansi. Soon after the maharaja died, he offered Rani a pension and ordered her to leave the Jhansi fort. Rani listened to the order delivered to her by a British officer and responded, "Jhansi is mine. I won't give it up." Those present reported that she was "white with rage."

Jhansi fort

British writer and colonial administrator Meadows Taylor, who met Rani of Jhansi, left us this description of her appearance: "She was fair and handsome, with a noble presence and a resolute, even stern expression... She wore a small cap of bright-colored scarlet silk with a string of pearls and rubies, and around her neck a diamond necklace sparkled, of not less value than a lakh (= 100 thousand) of rupees at least. Her belt was embroidered with gold, and in it were stuck two elaborately carved silver-mounted pistols of Damascus make, together with small but elegantly shaped hand-dagger, the point of which, it was whispered, had been dipped in a subtle poison, so that a wound, however slight, must prove fatal. Instead of the usual skirt she wore a pair of loose trousers..."

The Indian Rebellion started in 1857 with the revolt of the sepoys, the native Indian troops in the service of the East India Company. The sepoys were outraged that they were being sent to fight for the British in Burma without the additional "foreign pay," plus their rifle cartridges had to be greased to slide into the rifle, and the grease was rumored to come from either beef (prohibited among the Hindus), or pork (prohibited among the Muslims). The civilian population of India was also ready to rebel. British rule destroyed the economy of Indian villages – their traditional trades and crafts. The British built the railways and flooded Indian shops with European textiles and household goods, putting weavers, blacksmiths, and many other craftspeople out of business. Once the rebellion erupted, thousands of sepoys marched across India, taking forts and slaughtering British garrisons.

Jhansi was also overrun – by the rebels, and by the criminals the rebels released from jails. They besieged the Jhansi fort with about 60 British officials of the East India Company inside – with their wives and kids.

The British Hodson's Cavalry Regiment was made up of Sikh fighters from Punjab recruited by the British to suppress the Indian Rebellion of 1857

In his book *My Travels*, Indian author and Hindu priest Vishnubhat Godse, who witnessed the rebellion, says the British, cornered in the fort, reached out to Rani with this message: "It seems certain that tomorrow the worst will happen to us. We suggest that you take charge of your kingdom and hold it, along with the adjoining territory, until British authority is re-established. We shall be eternally grateful if you will also protect our lives." Rani got in touch with the rebels and helped negotiate the surrender of the British. They were promised that they would be let go if they opened the fort gates. But as the British came out of the fort, the sepoys received an order from one of the rebellion leaders to put all the Europeans to death. And they did. The rebels killed all their captives, including women and children.

This massacre was blamed on Rani, and the British turned against her. But for now they were busy chasing the rebels, and Rani had time to prepare for war. She ordered the construction of a foundry (metal-casting factory) to produce cannons and cannonballs, fortified the city, and stored food in case of a siege. Jhansi stood on a mountain. Its walls were constructed of granite, 16-20 feet (5-6m) thick, and its tall towers were equipped with brand-new cannons. Rani's volunteer army counted 14 thousand men and women. She set an example for her troops by leading an athletic lifestyle. Every day before breakfast she exercised by lifting weights and wrestling.

Meanwhile the British succeeded in suppressing the Indian Rebellion. They captured Delhi. The last Mughal emperor who sided with the rebels became a prisoner. His sons were shot dead after they surrendered to the British. In March of 1858 the East India Company's troops arrived at the walls of Jhansi and demanded its surrender. Rani refused. The British began bombarding the city. The defenders of Jhansi returned fire, and sent a messenger to Rani's childhood friend Tatya Tope, one of the leaders of the rebellion, asking him for help. Tope came with the force of 20 thousand and lit a huge bonfire on a hill to signal his arrival. Rani answered by firing the fort cannons. However, in the battle that followed, Tope couldn't overcome the British who blocked his approach to Jhansi. After 10 days of non-stop bombardment, the walls of Jhansi were badly damaged. In one area, where there was a breach, the British used bundles of grass to build a ramp, climbed up the wall and entered the city. Rani led 1500 of her soldiers to stop the enemy in hand-to-hand combat, but her forces were overwhelmed and chased back into the Jhansi fort. According to a legend, with Damodar Rao, the child-maharaja tied to her back with a silk scarf, Rani jumped down from the city wall on horseback, and escaped.

Through the 19th and most of the 20th centuries, the historical narrative about the Indian Rebellion was dominated by the British perspective. The stories of massacres of Europeans that occurred during the uprising were so vividly described in European press, and so graphically portrayed by European artists, that history books in Europe, America, and India heavily focused on the cruelty of the rebels, while the "other side of the story" was hardly ever told. Indian historian R.C.Majumdar wrote about this while discussing the siege of Kanpur (Cawnpore) where surrendering British military, their wives, and children were killed by the rebels: "While every schoolboy both in India and England reads about the cruel massacre of English men, women and children at Cawnpore, very few outside the circle of historians of modern India have any knowledge of the massacre, in cold blood, of Indian men, women and children, a hundred times the number of those that perished at Cawnpore."

"The storming of Jhansi" a vintage book illustration; Below: Rani of Jhansi on a 1953 movie poster and the monument to Rani in Solapur, India

This perspective is illustrated by Vishnubhat Godse who survived the siege of Jhansi. After the British captured Jhansi, they slaughtered its defenders and large numbers of civilians, burned the royal library, and looted the temple of goddess Lakshmi. "A Brahmin family who maintained a sacrificial fire were our neighbours," writes Vishnubhat Godse. "Two white soldiers accompanied by four Indian sepoys broke into his house. The whites went straight into the room reserved for the sacred fire which was covered with baskets. The whites kicked the baskets and saw heaps of ashes under them. They suspected that the Brahmin had hidden his valuables in the ashes and so they put in their hands to pull them out. Their hands were burnt and they were so infuriated they instantly killed the Brahmin, his brother, and his son. In all, they killed eleven people in that house and took away whatever little gold and silver they could lay their hands on... The English soldiers broke into houses and hunted out people hidden in barns, rafters and dark corners... Some tried to hide in haystacks but the pitiless demons set the haystacks on fire and hundreds were burned alive... If anybody jumped into a well the European soldiers shot him through the head as soon as he bobbed out of the water for breath."

After the fall of Jhansi, Rani of Jhansi fought alongside Tatya Tope, leading her own troops. British General Hugh Rose, who commanded the British forces, wrote about her, "The Rani was remarkable for her bravery, cleverness and perseverance. Her generosity to her subordinates was unlimited. These qualities, combined with her rank, made her the most dangerous of the rebel leaders."

Rani perished in a battle near the city of Gwalior. There are different accounts of her death. Most likely she was wounded in a sword fight and died in the rebel camp. Ramchandra Vinayak, an Indian diplomat who traveled with the British troops, reported, "At the time of the engagement the lady was present on the battlefield where she received a sabre blow which killed her. All people call her the bravest fighter." British major-general O.T. Burne compared Rani with the French heroine Joan of Arc, "This Indian Joan of Arc was dressed in a red jacket, trousers, and white turban. She wore a pearl necklace... As she lay mortally wounded in her tent, she ordered the pearls to be distributed among her troops. The whole rebel army mourned her loss."

A 19th-century portrait by an unknown Indian artist

SWAMI VIVEKANANDA
1863 – 1902

Swami Vivekananda was the first Indian thinker and spiritual teacher to present the wealth of Hindu philosophy and traditions to America and Europe through his lectures on Hinduism in the 1890s. He also brought Yoga to the West! He was India's first ever "spiritual ambassador" to the Western world. Having traveled extensively both in India and in the West, Vivekanda also sought to identify the best features of European social order, and promoted adopting these into Indian society. Swami Vivekananda was a monk and is widely viewed by Hindu believers as a saint.

Swami Vivekananda's birth name was Narendra. His father was an attorney practicing law at the Calcutta High Court. He came from an aristocratic Bengali family, and never had any interest in philosophy or religion. But he taught his kids compassion. One day when Narendra asked his dad why he was giving money to a family member who had lost his job and was often drunk, the response was, "How can you understand the great misery of human life? When you realize the depths of men's suffering, you will sympathize with those unfortunates who try to forget their sorrows, even only for a short while." Narendra's mother was raising 5 kids, and it's from her that he picked up curiosity about spirituality and religious traditions. In her free time his mom sat sewing and singing the great Indian epic poems, the Ramayana and the Mahabharata, from which she knew large portions by heart. Narendra never forgot his mother's advice: "Always follow the truth. Very often you may have to suffer injustice or unpleasant consequences for holding to the truth, but you must not, under any circumstances, abandon it."

Narendra excelled at school. In college he studied Indian and European philosophy and history in depth. Narendra's teachers and friends were stunned at his memory. He was able to quote a few pages of a book at a time! He also taught himself speed reading. While in college, Narendra started his own spiritual search and was advised to study with Sri Ramakrishna, a Hindu monk and guru who believed in the unity of all spiritual traditions and taught that all religions of the world lead to one God, but in different ways.

Ramakrishna

When Narendra visited Ramakrishna, he asked the monk, "Sir, have you seen God?" "Yes, I have seen God," replied Ramakrishna. "I see Him as I see you here, only more clearly. God can be seen. One can talk to him. But who cares for God? People shed torrents of tears for their wives, children, wealth, and property, but who weeps for the vision of God? If one cries sincerely for God, one can surely see Him."

Sri

The Sanskrit word "Sri," when used with Hindu names, means "holy," "respected," "admired." It is often added to the names of famous gurus.

It took Narendra some time to appreciate Ramakrishna's mystical experiences and teaching. Narendra didn't feel he needed a spiritual guide, a "go-between" him and God. Annoyed at Narendra's criticism of the worship of Hindu gods, Ramakrishna once asked Narendra, "Why do you even come here if you do not accept Kali [Hindu goddess], my mother?" "Must I accept her just because I visit you? I come because I love you," answered Narendra. "This boy has no faith in the various forms of God," Ramakrishna complained to his disciples. "He tells me that my visions are pure imagination. But he is a fine lad of pure mind. He does not accept anything without direct evidence. He has studied a lot and has good judgement."

In 1884 Narendra's father died, and his family was left with no income. They were deeply in debt and began slipping into poverty. Knowing that Ramakrishna focused much of his worship on the Hindu goddess Kali, Narendra asked Ramakrishna to pray to Kali that he finds a job and income. "Go yourself to her temple and pray," responded Ramakrishna. "Prostrate yourself before her image, and pray to her for your needs. Your prayer will be answered." At the temple, Narendra was filled with amazement as he reflected on the great mysteries of faith and the secrets of the universe. He asked the goddess for wisdom, forgetting to pray for a job and money. Soon he realized that the material aspects of life and the privileges they offered – income, property, comfort, social status – had very little meaning to him. In 1886 Ramakrishna died. Narendra and a few of Ramakrishna's students formed a ***monastic order*** – a society of monks – whose goal was to live in accordance with Ramakrishna's teaching.

When they took monastic vows, Narendra received a new name – Swami Vivekananda. "Vivekananda" is formed from two Sanskrit words – viveka ("pursuit of wisdom") and ananda ("happiness") – "the happiness of discovering wisdom." However, Vivekananda came to the conclusion that the best way to worship God was to help people by saving them from poverty and ignorance, while also teaching them about God. He was now on a mission that was incompatible with the quiet life of a monastery. He had to "do something," go somewhere. So, in 1888 Swami Vivekananda started his travels. For 5 years he went around India, living on occasional donations and mixing with people of all castes, ethnic groups, and religions.

One day he was invited to visit the court of a local maharaja. "You are a scholar. Why do you travel around like a beggar?" asked the maharaja. "And why do you spend all your days with your European friends hunting as if you have no duties?" responded Vivekananda. Irritated, the maharaja, who had received the British education and looked down on the Hindu religious tradition, continued by criticising the worship of gods' images. "They are nothing but stone, clay, and metal," he concluded. Years ago Narenda would have agreed with him, but his studies and spiritual experiences had brought him to respect every expression of faith. He calmly pointed to the maharaja's portrait on the wall decorated with gold jewelry and adorned with flowers, and addressed the royal prime minister, "How about you take this down and maybe spit on this image once or twice?" The court fell silent in horror. Then the Swami turned to the maharaja and explained that even though his portrait wasn't the maharaja himself, it represented the king to his subjects and reminded them who was the boss. Similarly, the images of gods and saints channel the thoughts of believers toward God and help them focus on the divine presence in the world. The maharaja agreed with him and apologized.

One day, while traveling, Swami Vivekananda shared a railway compartment with two Englishmen. They were rude fellows, and noticing his cheap worn clothes they figured he didn't speak English, and amused themselves by cracking jokes about him in his presence. Then, suddenly, they heard him talk to a British train conductor in perfect English. "Why didn't you stop us when we made fun of you?" they asked the Swami. "Because this is not the first time I've been around fools," said Vivekananda who never hesitated to deal out penalties to those who deserved them. But in the town of Khetri, in Rajasthan, Vivekananda himself was taught a lesson he never forgot. He was invited by the Maharaja of Khetri to an evening of entertainment in which one of the court's "dancing girls" was to perform song and dance. As a monk, Vivekananda was not supposed to enjoy 'impure' experiences, such as dancing shows and songs about falling in love, beautiful girls, broken hearts, and such. Plus "dancing girls" certainly didn't have a good reputation. So he spent some time with the maharaja, but as soon as the "dancing girl" arrived, he headed for the door. The "dancing girl" was disappointed, and being a talented poetess, she improvised a song:

Look not, my lord, upon my sins,
You, whose fame is open-mindedness...
Sacred is the water of the Yamuna River,
Foul is the water in a roadside ditch,
Yet all the waters are sanctified alike
When they flow into the holy stream of the Ganges...

Vivekananda was moved and confirmed in his deepest belief that in the eyes of God there is no distinction between "pure" and "impure." Unable to hold back tears, he stayed for the concert and told the singer, "Mother, I am guilty. I was about to show you disrespect by refusing to come to this room. But your song awakened my consciousness."

"A dancing girl" – a vintage photo, India, late 19th century

Travel around India opened Swami Vivekananda's eyes to the disastrous poverty in many regions of the country. He set himself the goal of discovering the methods of social and economic improvement used by the Western world, where living standards were higher. "I have travelled all over India," he told his friends. "But it was agony to me, my brothers, to see with my own eyes the terrible poverty of the masses, and I could not restrain my tears! It is now my firm conviction that to preach religion amongst them, without first trying to remove their poverty and suffering, is futile. It is for this reason – to find means for the salvation of the poor of India – that I am going to America."
The Maharaja of Khetri bought the Swami a first-class ticket on a steamship leaving for China, and, finally, he made his way to Canada and the United States.

In the US, Swami Vivekananda's destination was Chicago. At the Chicago World's Fair they held the Parliament of Religions – a gathering of over 7000 representatives of many religious communities from around the world. Vivekananda was scheduled to address the Parliament of Religions, but he was so nervous, he didn't sleep for days and prayed non-stop.

When he was called to speak, he asked to postpone his presentation. "My heart was fluttering and my tongue nearly dried up," he recalled. Finally when he faced the audience to make his speech, the first words he said were, "Sisters and brothers of America!" Suddenly all the 7000+ people in front of him rose from their chairs and applauded him for – what seemed to be forever! (Witnesses said it was 2 minutes.) The simplicity and warmth of his words contrasted sharply with most speeches that had an "official" feel about them. The rest of Swami Vivekananda's address echoed the main goal of the gathering – to find points on which most religions of the world agree. For example, making the case that different faiths are just different paths to discover God, he quoted the old Hindu hymn praising Shiva, "Whoever comes to me, by whatever path, I reach him. All men are struggling through paths that in the end all lead to me." There was more deafening applause, and the next day Swami Vivekananda woke up a celebrity!

Newspapers in the US and Europe reported that he was the "greatest figure," the most influential presence at the Parliament of Religions. The New York Herald declared, "After hearing him we feel how foolish it is to send missionaries to this learned nation, India." The Boston Evening Post reported, "At the Parliament of Religions they kept Vivekananda until the end of the program to make people stay till the end of the session... People sat smiling and expectant, waiting for an hour or two to listen to Vivekananda for fifteen minutes. The chairman knew the old rule of keeping the best until the last." Wealthy people lined up to meet the famous guru and thousands of dollars in donations were offered to him. The success was bittersweet. "What do I care about fame when my motherland remains sunk in utmost poverty?" he complained. "When millions of us die because we don't have even a handful of rice, and here they spend millions on their personal comfort! Who will raise the people of India? Who will give them bread?" In the following years Swami Vivekananda delivered hundreds of lectures at universities, churches, and religious societies across the US and in Europe. There were more invitations to events than he could attend. Harvard University and Columbia University offered him positions of the chairman of their Eastern Philosophy departments, but Vivekananda didn't accept these prestigious invitations feeling that they didn't fit his calling as a monk and a traveling guru.

At one of Swami Vivekananda's lectures he met an American woman who came up to him and said, "I want to marry you." "Why?" asked Swami Vivekananda. "I am deeply impressed with your intellect and personality," she answered. "I want to have a brilliant son like you." "We could certainly get married," said the Swami, "but raising a child is a very long process, and there is no guarantee that the child will grow up just the way you want him to be. So I have a better idea for you. Why won't you adopt me as your son? You will be my proud mother instantly." They both laughed and the woman became one of Vivekananda's students. Vivekananda wasn't always welcoming and humorous. Sometimes his speeches rang with anger at the abuse India suffered at the hands of European colonial powers, and the fact that European and American Christians failed to raise their voice against colonialism. "You train and pay men to do what?" he asked. "To come over to my country and curse and abuse my ancestors, my religion... They walk near a temple and say, 'You idol-worshippers, you will go to hell!' ... And if I just touch you with the least bit of criticism, you cry: 'Do not touch us! We are Americans... We are sensitive plants'... You are not Christians. No, as a nation you are not. Go back to Christ. Go back to him who had nowhere to lay down his head. Yours is a religion preached in the name of luxury!"

Yoga

In 1896 Swami Vivekananda published his book "Raja Yoga" that presented the ancient Hindu yoga philosophy to Western audiences. The book was an instant success. The Sanskrit word "yoga" has the same Indo-European root as the English word "yoke." A yoke is a wooden bar that holds the necks of the animals that pull a plough together. The original meaning of this root is "to restrict, to constrain." The ancient yoga tradition focused on meditation and restricting, limiting one's attention to the object of meditation – a religious or spiritual idea. Swami Vivekananda's book "Raja Yoga" presented only this spiritual part of the yoga teaching. Later in the 20th century Indian gurus introduced their Western audiences to yoga as a physical practice based on "asanas" – postures, poses. Eventually the Western versions of yoga became a physical fitness discipline and a method of stress relief.

Swami Vivekananda traveled to England to lecture on Hinduism and yoga. In his letters he reported, "No one ever landed on English soil feeling more hatred in his heart for any race than I did for the English... Now there is none who loves the English people more than I do...The English are not as bright as the Americans, but once you touch their heart, it is yours forever... they are, of all nations, least jealous of each other and that is why they dominate the world. They have solved the secret of obedience without slavish cringing..." He also wrote, "The British Empire with all its evils is the greatest machine that ever existed for the dissemination of ideas. I mean to put my ideas in the centre of this machine, and it will spread them all over the world. Of course, all great work is slow and the difficulties are too many, especially as we, Hindus, are a conquered race. Yet that is the very reason why it is bound to work, for spiritual ideals have always come from the downtrodden."

In 1897 Swami Vivekananda returned to India and traveled around by train giving lectures. His fame extended to every corner of India, and as he traveled people would gather by railroad stations and sit on the train tracks, forcing the train to stop so that they could listen to a few words from Swami Vivekananda! His message to his Indian listeners was different from what he said in the West. In India he talked about ways to eliminate the caste system, raise common people from poverty, and put an end to British colonial rule. In one of his speeches he said, "What our country now wants is muscles of iron and nerves of steel, gigantic will, which nothing can resist... If you have faith in your mythological gods, and in all the gods which foreigners have introduced into your midst, and still have no faith in yourselves, there is no salvation for you. Have faith in yourselves and stand upon that faith! Why is it that we, three hundred and thirty million people, have been ruled for the last thousand years by any and every handful of foreigners? Because they had faith in themselves and we didn't... When one of our poor fellows is murdered or ill-treated by an Englishman, howling rises all over the country... Who is responsible for it all? Not the English. It is we who are responsible for all our degradation. Our aristocratic ancestors went on treading the common people of our country underfoot till they became helpless, till the poor forgot that they were human beings."

On the day he died Swami Vivekananda spent three hours in the morning meditating, and the afternoon – teaching Sanskrit grammar and yoga philosophy to his students. Then he left for his room, closed the door and passed away during his evening meditation.

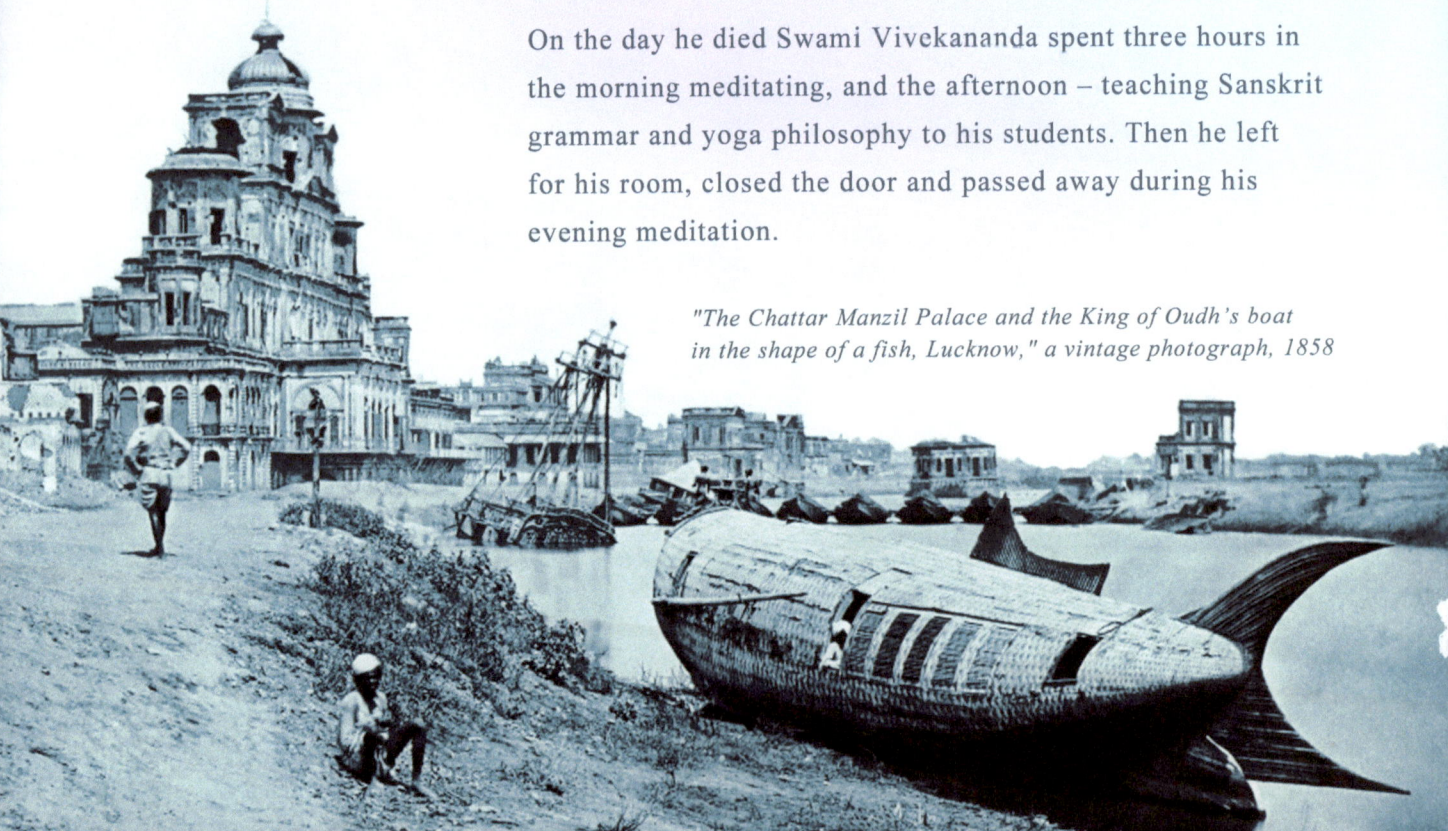

"The Chattar Manzil Palace and the King of Oudh's boat in the shape of a fish, Lucknow," a vintage photograph, 1858

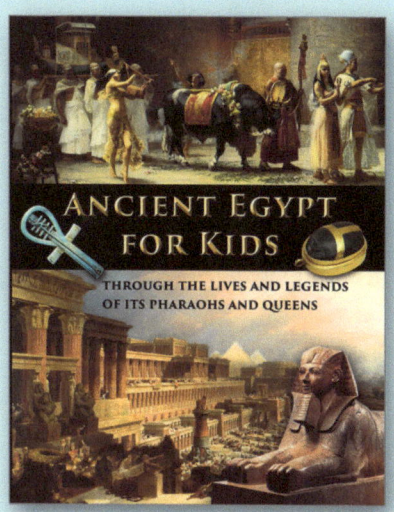
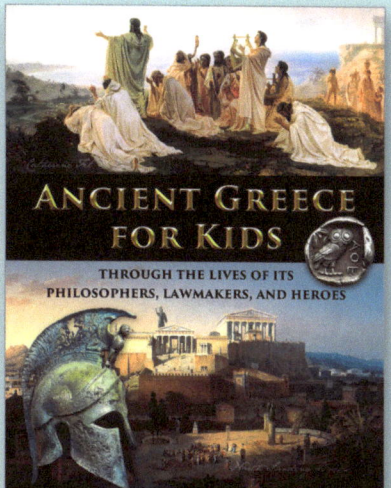
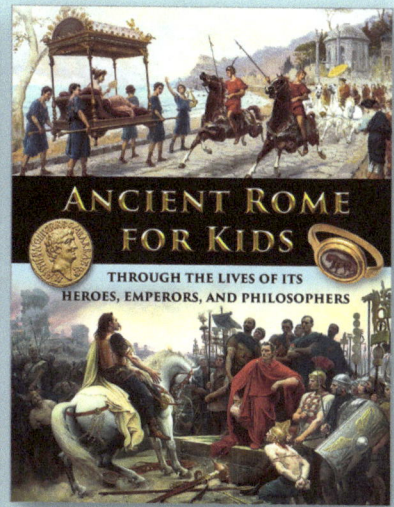
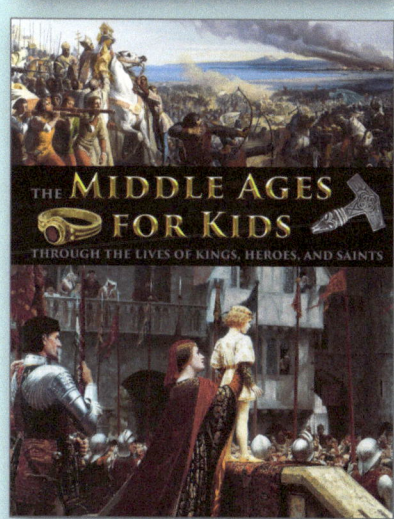
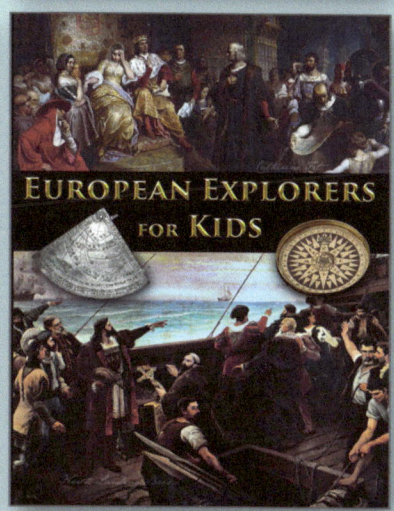
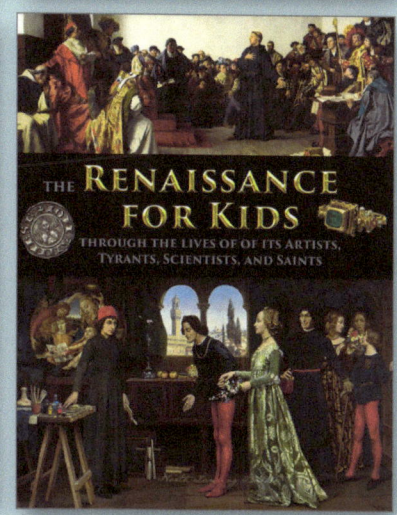
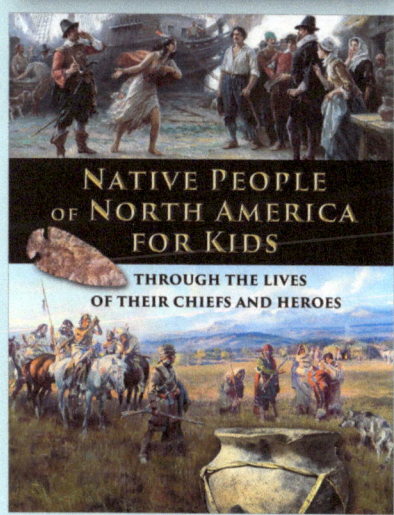
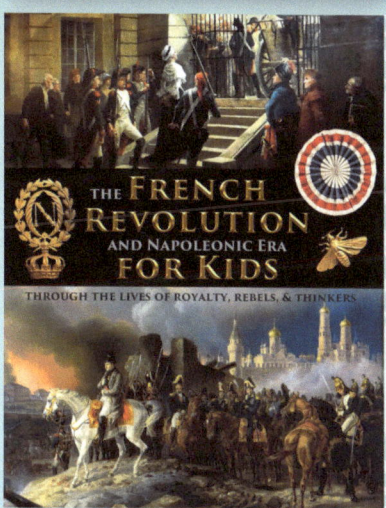
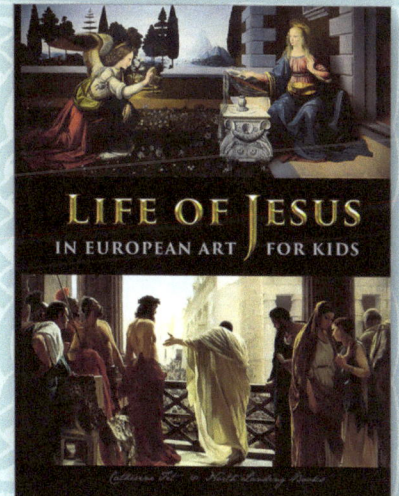

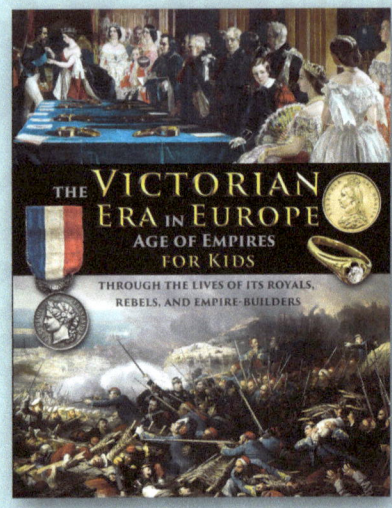
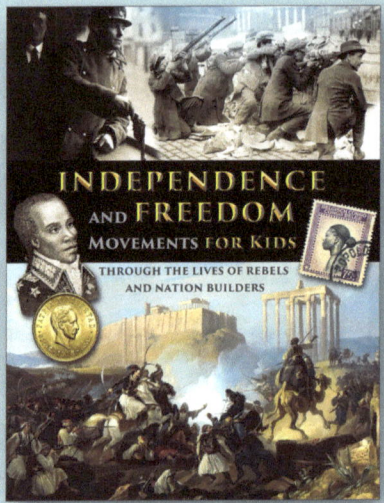
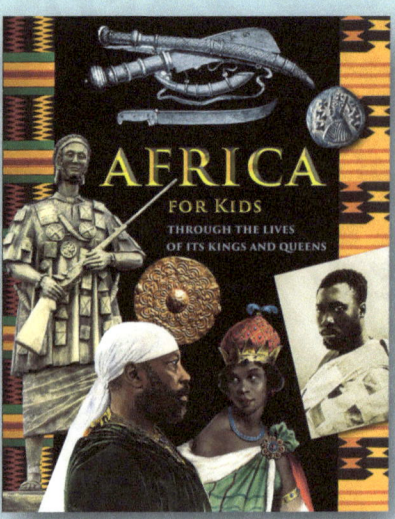

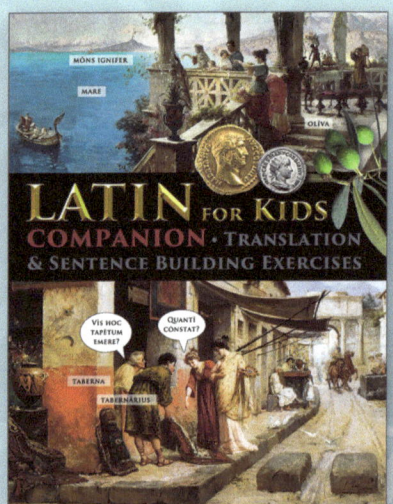

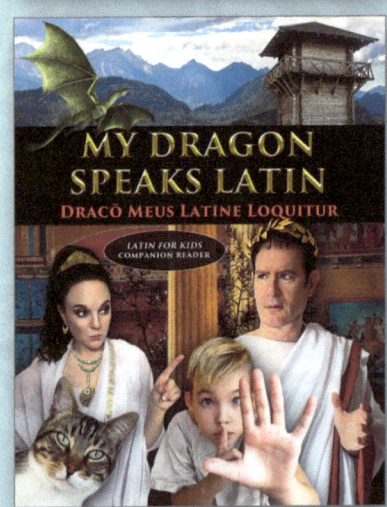
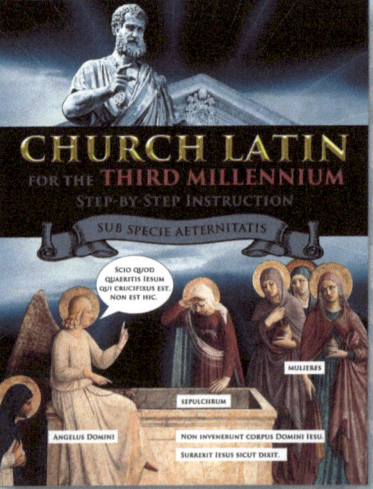

www.ingramcontent.com/pod-product-compliance
Lightning Source LLC
LaVergne TN
LVHW071656060526
838201LV00037B/366